MODELLING TUNNELS, EMBANKMENTS, WALLS AND FENCES

FOR MODEL RAILWAYS

MODELLING TUNNELS, EMBANKMENTS, WALLS AND FENCES
FOR MODEL RAILWAYS

DAVID TISDALE

THE CROWOOD PRESS

First published in 2017 by
The Crowood Press Ltd
Ramsbury, Marlborough
Wiltshire SN8 2HR

www.crowood.com

British Library Cataloguing-in-Publication Data
A catalogue record for this book is available from the British Library.

ISBN 978 1 78500 328 8

Typeset by Servis Filmsetting Ltd, Stockport, Cheshire
Printed and bound in India by Parkson's Graphics

CONTENTS

PREFACE AND ACKNOWLEDGEMENTS

PREFACE

The concept for this book came from observing many layouts at numerous model railway shows across the country. When Crowood presented me with a number of possible subjects for a new title, the idea of writing about some of the key elements of railway infrastructure leapt out. I am fascinated by railway engineering, both historic and modern, and this interest inspired this book.

This book was written as a guide for both the beginner and seasoned railway modeller, to provide helpful hints and tips for the creation of more visually accurate and realistic railway infrastructure on a model layout. Careful construction of a model

Fig. 1   The use of realistic railway infrastructure enhances the appearance of a model railway; this is 'Leamington Spa' in O-gauge by Pete Waterman.

railway, with prototypically modelled infrastructure and landscape, contributes to a more believable representation of the real world. Realistic modelling of the infrastructure and the ways in which the railway relates to the landscape is the factor that will differentiate your model railway from a train set.

I have constructed a number of layouts in various scale and gauge combinations, including O-16.5, OO, OO9 and N-gauge, both on an individual basis and as part of a team at my local model railway club, Jersey Model Railway Club. With this experience in mind, I thought it might be beneficial to other railway modellers if I could provide some tips and guidance based on my experience, for the creation of tunnels, embankments, walls and fences for the 'average railway modeller' (to borrow a well-known phrase from *Railway Modeller*).

All of the techniques described in this book have been utilized by me on my own layouts, or on club layouts, unless otherwise stated. My colleagues Derek Lawrence, Tim Pollard and Pete Waterman have all been kind enough to allow me to take a few pictures of their own layouts to use as examples in this book. I hope therefore to be able to offer my thoughts on what does and does not work for me and encourage you, the reader, to try out some of these ideas on your own layouts.

ACKNOWLEDGEMENTS

I would like to convey my thanks to my fellow railway modellers at the Jersey Model Railway Club for their support, advice and encouragement during the preparation of this book. In particular, I would like to thank Derek Lawrence and Tim Pollard for allowing me to photograph their layouts to illustrate some of the features described in this book.

A special thank you is also due to our Honorary Club President Pete Waterman for allowing me to visit his fantastic Leamington Spa layout and use a couple of photographs of this layout as examples of what can be achieved in realistic infrastructure modelling in O-gauge.

Finally, I would especially like to thank my wife and family for tolerating my model railway stuff all over the house and for their support and encouragement during the preparation of this book.

David Tisdale
St Ouen, Jersey

CHAPTER ONE

RAILWAY INFRASTRUCTURE IN THE LANDSCAPE

The construction of railways with steam locomotive traction began in the early nineteenth century and a fundamental aspect of the development of the railways was the establishment of appropriate infrastructure to allow the railway lines to extend from one location to the next. Generally speaking, the infrastructure had to be designed to allow relatively easy movement of the locomotive and rolling stock along the track.

Railways were built to serve communities and the routes did not necessarily follow a straight line between two points. Aspiring railway companies, their supporters and financiers, as well as local landowners and other vested interests, all had their own reasons for influencing the course of the route, either to keep railways away from their land, or conversely to bring the railway close to their village, town, city or industrial site, so that they might benefit from the railway's presence and communication with the wider world. As a consequence, many of the original railway routes tended to wind their way between population centres and industrial sites and not necessarily by the most direct or efficient route.

Fig. 2   Railway expansion provided Victorian workers with the opportunity for day trips and holidays to the coast, leading to the development of stations and resorts such as Dawlish, UK.

The railways were seen as a stimulus to development of both population centres and industrial sites, such as mines, quarries, harbours, iron works, mills and manufacturing sites. The coming of the railways had a profound effect on society and the countryside. The railways facilitated the increased exploitation and export of raw materials and manufactured goods, as well as leading to a massive social revolution by enabling the movement of people to urban areas to work at the factories and industrial sites.

As the railways developed, the mass movement of people – for both social and recreational purposes – became more common. The railways afforded huge numbers of people, who had previously been confined by poor transport links to their local area, the opportunity to travel and experience other parts of the country. Most notably in the late nineteenth century and early twentieth century, this was associated with the development of the concept of 'a day at the seaside'.

Fig. 4 The construction of the Channel Tunnel was one of the single largest railway projects in the history of the UK system; here, a section through one of the running tunnels is recreated at The National Railway Museum, York, UK.

Fig. 3 Commuter train at the central station, Florence, Italy; urban railways and commuting represent the modern way of life for many.

Fig. 5 *The Old Red Sandstone cliffs of the South Devon coast, UK, presented a major geological challenge to the development of the railway.*

Despite the best efforts of a certain doctor in the 1960s, the railways continue to provide a critical transport network across the UK, transporting freight and people for both business and leisure reasons. Recently, the network has seen the development of the Channel Tunnel and high-speed rail link (HS1) from central London to mainland Europe, as well as intensive development of new rail infrastructure to serve the large population centres. That infrastructure is only now starting to see significant investment to upgrade and expand a system that still relies in many places on an infrastructure that was laid down by the pioneer railway engineers during the nineteenth century.

INFLUENCE OF THE NATURAL LANDSCAPE

Whilst early railway development was predicated on the requirement to improve transportation links, and to speed up the time taken to move people and goods between points, the route of each railway line between the known points was also heavily influenced by the topography through which it had to travel. The physical challenges presented by the landscape formed part of the early planning and assessment of route viability. The local geology, or rock types, as well as the shape and form of the landscape, referred to as its geomorphology, were critical elements that had to be assessed in route selection by the early railway engineers.

GEOLOGY

The local geology of the area through which the railway was planned would be one of the most important physical constraints that the early railway engineers had to tackle. The rock type influenced a number of critical aspects of the railway line construction, from the selection of a route to provide a solid foundation for the track bed, to the choice of method to build the railway through the landscape using a combination of cuttings, tunnels, embankments and bridges or viaducts.

The local rock types in many areas were also used as the raw materials to form the railway infrastructure. Along railway routes, stone was often quarried to build features such as bridges and viaducts, or clay may have been dug and used to form embankments.

In areas of hard rock – for example, the distinctive Old Red Sandstone in Devon – the engineers had to find innovative solutions. On the famous coastal section near Dawlish in Devon, the railway was in places established on ledges cut in to the rock, and tunnels were driven through the headlands in order to thread the railway through.

At the other extreme is the example of east Norfolk, where the railway line between Norwich and Great Yarmouth crosses the flat low-lying coastal plain. There was no hard rock support for the railway track bed; most of the route of the railway in this area had to be formed across waterlogged and low-lying marshes. In this instance the track bed was supported across the former coastal marshes on a low embankment, to keep it above the flood level. On this route the railway engineers had to look at alternative ways of supporting the railway infrastructure, including the use of timber baulks laid on the soft clay ground to support the railway embankment.

GEOMORPHOLOGY

The form of the landscape through which the railway line passes is, naturally, a function of the geology. The shape of the landscape is a function of a number of physical processes, such as wind, water and ice (glaciers), which have carved, eroded and deposited the underlying geology to form the shapes that are visible today. The influence of man has also to a lesser extent helped form the shape of the land in the last 100 years or so, but at the time when railway construction began, this impact was less noticeable.

The geomorphology determined a number of key elements of the railway construction. The presence of hills and valleys along the route of the railways presented physical challenges to railway engineers that would have had a time and cost impact on the development of the railway line.

Fig. 6   The Settle and Carlisle route negotiates some of the most dramatic scenery on the UK railway network. It threw up some enormous engineering challenges, necessitating the construction of tunnels, embankments and viaducts.

Many routes were selected to reduce where possible the need for the expensive and time-consuming construction of engineering infrastructure, such as tunnels, bridges and viaducts, or creating earthworks such as cuttings and embankments. However, on some routes and in some locations there would have been no choice, which has resulted in the legacy of some excellent Victorian engineering, including Brunel's Royal Albert Bridge at Saltash and Box Tunnel, and the equally impressive grand viaducts, tunnels and embankments on the Settle to Carlisle line of the former Midland Railway.

ENGINEERING CHALLENGES IN EARLY RAILWAY DEVELOPMENT

ENGINEERING PIONEERS

The advent of the railways led to the rise of the brilliant railway engineer. There was a need for visionary technicians to plan, design and then construct the substantial infrastructure of the railway system, much of which still forms the foundations of the modern railway network. Engineers such as Isambard Kingdom Brunel, father and son George and Robert Stephenson, Joseph Locke and Thomas Telford are just some of the key people responsible for the development of the Victorian railway networks.

The works of George and Robert Stephenson in the north-east of England included the construction of the Stockton & Darlington Railway, the first public railway in the world, which kick-started the rapid development of the railway infrastructure of the UK during the Victorian period.

As a Great Western Railway fan and an engineer myself, I find the railway engineering exploits of Brunel particularly inspiring. One of the best-known Victorian pioneers, Brunel was responsible for the significant development of the railway infrastructure of the Great Western Railway. His broad-gauge (7 feet and ¼ inch) Bristol to London railway, which included the hugely impressive Box Tunnel, was constructed to minimize the impact of

gradients and curves, to accommodate the ever-increasing speed of the trains. His other notable railway engineering feats included working with his father on the construction of one of the first tunnels beneath the River Thames and the development of the tunnelling shield as a construction method to protect workers at the tunnel face. This tunnel now forms part of the London Underground network and is still in use today. The tunnel shield technique was the forerunner of modern tunnel-boring machines.

Perhaps one of Brunel's most iconic railway engineering projects was the construction of the Royal Albert Bridge over the Tamar, west of Plymouth, which carries the railway between Devon and Cornwall. In the same part of the UK, the construction of the series of tunnels to carry first his experimental atmospheric railway and then, when that failed, a more traditional steam locomotive-powered railway line between Exeter and Teignmouth, along the east coast of Devon at Dawlish, is perhaps one of the most scenic settings in the country.

Another first for Brunel was the construction of the Severn Tunnel, which, when completed, was the longest railway tunnel in the UK, at over 4 miles (around 6.5km) long. It remained a record-holder for over 100 years, until the construction of the tunnels as part of the HS1 route into London.

To paraphrase the words of Biddle & Nock (1983), the creation of the railway infrastructure during the Victorian period – including, among other things, the development of the attendant tunnels, cuttings, embankments and trackside buildings – all together comprised one of the greatest construction projects ever undertaken in the UK. The end result was probably the most significant change that had ever occurred on the face of the country, happening faster and more completely than anything before – and, some might argue, since.

By the end of the nineteenth century the UK had some 19,000 miles of track, 9,000 stations, 60,000 bridges, 1,000 tunnels, and hundreds of viaducts and trackside buildings, ranging from warehouses and engine sheds to signal boxes and crossing keepers' cottages (after Biddle & Nock, 1983).

Fig. 7 One of Brunel's greatest railway engineering projects was the construction of the Royal Albert Bridge, completed in 1859, over the River Tamar at Saltash near Plymouth, UK.

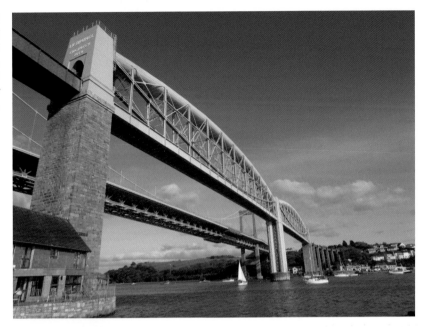

Fig. 8 The coastal route between Teignmouth and Dawlish in Devon, UK, was another feat of Victorian railway engineering pioneers.

TRACK BED

The railway engineer's job was, and still is, to ensure that the track bed is constructed in such a way as to optimize train movement. The aim should be to make the ride and route as easy as possible for the rolling stock, taking out significant changes in gradient or at least reducing them to an acceptable trafficable level without resorting to additional traction measures such as cog-drive systems. On some routes, this is not possible – as can be seen on a number of routes on the Swiss railway system and in the UK on the Snowdon Mountain Railway – but these are the exceptions rather than the norm.

Fig. 9   The Snowdon Mountain Railway is one of the few examples in the UK where trains have to make use of a central rack-and-pinion cog system to aid traction up the steep gradients of the track bed.

Building a relatively level track bed, in order to smooth out the steeper gradients, necessitated the design and construction of engineering infrastructure, such as embankments, cuttings, tunnels, bridges and viaducts. The focus of this book is on two of these infrastructure solutions: embankments and tunnels. Embankments are used to build up the track bed across low-lying areas, while tunnels are used to get the track bed through physical barriers such as hills and mountains. They are also used to traverse urban areas, where land use is much denser and land values are higher, and burying underneath is the only viable option.

The planning of a model railway layout has already been covered in great depth by many authors who are more qualified than I am, so their work is recommended for general layout planning guidance. For advice on planning with specific reference to the formation of the track bed and the creation of the necessary infrastructure required to support that track bed, see Chapter 2.

GRADIENTS

Reference to Scott (1972) indicates that, in the case of the Great Western Railway, the track bed gradient design was broken down into three classifications in order to apply a description to the routes:

- Shallow gradients: track bed between 1 in 340 and 1 in 660;
- Steeper gradients: track bed <1 in 100;
- Very steep gradients: track bed less <1 in 50.

This grouping of gradients is for use on the prototype and not for model railways, but it gives an indication of what needs to be considered when setting out a track bed on a model railway. Chapter 4 includes a section on calculating the length of track bed that will be needed to construct suitable gradients for a model railway, along with some examples for reference.

TUNNELLING

The use of tunnels by railway engineers was usually confined to areas where the track bed could not be easily accommodated via an alternative route on cuttings and/or embankments, or in an urban area where the only option through the area, without demolition of properties, was to tunnel beneath. However, in more modern late twentieth-century and early twenty-first-century railway engineering works, the use of tunnels is often adopted as a way of reducing the environmental impact of the railway on the landscape and to access areas that are already heavily developed, such as city centres.

Fig. 10 In urban areas, railways often use tunnels to access stations in the city centre, such as here at the central station in Hamburg, Germany.

One good example of a more recent use of tunnels is the route of HS1 in the southern part of the UK, connecting the Channel Tunnel with the international rail terminus at St Pancras Station in central London. Other examples would be the proposed HS2 route northwards from London and the Crossrail project in the south-east of the UK around London; these projects include a significant use of tunnels to take the railway development through urban areas, and, in the case of HS1 and HS2, areas of outstanding natural beauty, where the aim is to preserve the landscape for the future.

The environmental constraints that confront modern railway engineering works were less relevant during the nineteenth century and early twentieth century, when the bulk of the railway network of the UK was constructed by the Victorians. The use of tunnels was, and still is, an expensive option, both in terms of time and money to build and also in terms of the risk to the people building the railway.

Chapter 3 covers in more detail some worked examples of the construction of tunnels, and considers features such as wing walls and portals. It also looks at the types of materials used for lining of the tunnels; the use of ventilation shafts, in particular, with respect to tunnels in model form; and the need to consider how to access the tracks in a tunnel for track cleaning and recovery of derailed rolling stock.

Tunnels may be used on a model railway for a variety of purposes: for example, to act as a scenic break between different sections of a layout; to disguise the entrance or exit to a fiddle yard; or to hide sharp non-prototypical curves or corners in the track where the size of the layout baseboard is constrained by the place in which it is located.

EMBANKMENTS

Embankments have a number of uses as part of railway infrastructure. They can be used as an alternative to the construction of bridges and viaducts for a railway to cross a low-lying area. These types of structures are built to ensure that where possible the railway track bed is kept at a relatively flat or shallow gradient, to even out the rise and fall of the natural landscape. Embankments have also been used as a method of raising or lowering the track bed between running lines at different levels.

The use of embankments is widespread on the railway network and the structures have been formed from a variety of materials, often determined by the local availability of suitable materials (see the earlier comments about geology). For information on the construction and use of embankments, along with reference to examples, see Chapter 4.

Fig. 11 Embankments, such as this example on the Welshpool and Llanfair Caereinon Light Railway in Wales, carry railways across river flood plains or are used as alternatives to bridges across low-lying areas.

RAILWAY BOUNDARIES

Beyond the construction of the major railway infrastructure to support the track bed, consideration also needs to be given to the land belonging to the railway in which the infrastructure sits, and to the ways in which this land may be defined.

CONSTRUCTING WALLS

There are a number of different wall types that can be included on a layout, including boundary walls and engineering walls, which all form an important part of the railway infrastructure. Walls can be formed from a wide range of material types and their construction is covered in Chapter 5, together with some suggestions and methods of how they might be replicated in model form on a layout. The examples include ready-to-plant structures, construction of kits and scratch-building techniques.

INSTALLING FENCES

Different fence styles and types are covered in Chapter 6, along with information on how and where they might be used in the real world, and therefore

Fig. 12 Retaining walls and bridge abutments frame the western end to Llangollen Station, Wales, as it squeezes between the town and the river.

Fig. 13 At Buckfastleigh Station on the South Devon Railway, the many different fence types reflect the various phases of railway development and preservation.

how they might be applied to a model railway layout. A wide range of fence types is covered, with examples used to show how they can be recreated using ready-to-plant items, kits and scratch-building methods.

DETAILING MODEL INFRASTRUCTURE

The final chapter provides some ideas for detailing the infrastructure around the model railway, in order to bring the scene to life. The choice of detail may be governed by the intended setting, but there is no wrong or right way to do it; it is down to personal preference. The extra detail might include vegetation, people and animals for a rural-themed layout; an urban-themed layout might benefit from the addition of details such as litter, graffiti on walls, burnt-out cars and old shopping trolleys.

Each example has been constructed by me, either for one of my own layouts or as part of a club project. They are from both OO-gauge and N-gauge layouts, but the principles of each can be equally applied to other scales.

Fig. 14 The coal yard on my 'Llanfair & Meifod' OO-gauge layout: attention to detail helps create a realistic model railway.

CHAPTER TWO

ADDING REALISTIC INFRASTRUCTURE TO MODEL RAILWAYS

PLANNING A LAYOUT

There are a number of extremely helpful texts that cover the planning and building of model railway layouts in great detail, so there is no need to do that here. Two good references for baseboard design and construction are Nigel Burkin, who provides advice on layout construction and design techniques for model railways (Burkin, 2010), and Ron Pybus, who covers the design and building of baseboards (Pybus, 2015).

When planning a model railway layout, modellers nearly always start with a consideration of the track layout and, perhaps most importantly, a determination of what they want to achieve operationally from the layout. However, as well as the track and operational interest, it is equally important to plan the landscape in which the proposed model railway will be set. The landscape and scenery of the layout bring it alive as a representation of the real world and add that level of believability.

PROTOTYPE RESEARCH

If you are planning a layout based on a real location, it would be a good idea to try to obtain and review maps of the location for the period in which the model is to be set. For locations in the UK, there is a wealth of information available from old Ordnance Survey sheets, which can often be picked up from second-hand bookshops or charity shops. Some maps may be available online at a modest cost, or may be obtained from the Local Studies section of your local library (assuming it has not been closed!). If the subject area and timescale of your model are relatively recent, new maps can be purchased from good bookshops or online from a number of suppliers, as well as direct from Ordnance Survey in the UK.

In addition to contemporary maps, old photographs of the subject area can be informative and provide visual evidence for period features that may be added to the layout. In addition to historical photographic information, recent photographs, combined with a site visit if feasible and affordable, will also provide much valuable information, giving a feel for the local area and landscape in which the railway was/is set.

Rural Settings

In a rural setting, there are a number of features to observe and note during a site visit, including some or all of the following:

- The size and shape of hills and valleys and the angle of slopes – are they steep or shallow?
- The location of rivers and streams, which gives information about the drainage of the area; do bridges and culverts need to be included?
- The presence of rock outcrops gives an indication of the underlying geology and will help with an understanding of the shape of the landscape.
- The construction of property and field boundaries; if there are walls, are they drystone, dressed stone, rough stone, with or without mortar, or simple brick? If there are fences, what type of fence marks the railway boundary as well as property boundaries?
- Look at how the railway infrastructure sits in the landscape. Have cuttings or embankments been used? Are there small occupation bridges and/or grand stone viaducts marching across the scenery?

As a geologist and geotechnical engineer, this type of observation was part of my training and formed part of my job. Today, it is a habit that I find difficult to abandon as I travel around the country and it can be very beneficial in terms of coming up with ideas as to how to recreate scenes in model form. However, for

Fig. 15   A typical rural setting to the railway line; a wealth of landscape and scenic features can be replicated on a model railway to improve realism.

most railway modellers, just looking at a few of the basic items will give a good feel for the lie of the land or the topography and character of the area that you intend to represent.

Urban Settings

When considering modelling an urban setting, it is important to realize that some or all of the natural landscape features are likely to be buried, or at least masked by the development of the town or city. However, there are likely to be some features that remain identifiable, as well as characteristics and features that will be more specific to urban areas.

From an information-gathering perspective for modelling, there are a number of features to look out for during a site visit in an urban area:

- How has the urban development fitted into the landscape? For example, steeply sloping streets and the presence of retaining walls indicate that the area may have featured hills and valleys before being built up.
- The street names in the surrounding area can give clues to the landscape underlying the site; for example, Marsh Lane probably gets its name from an area that was poorly drained

before development and might therefore need culverts and drainage channels.
- Record the presence of embankments, tunnels and cuttings and how the railway has been built through the development.
- Look at the architectural styles of buildings that have been developed in the area around the railway and their relative ages; for example, all new buildings could indicate expansion of development or renewal of older buildings.
- Look at the buildings and land adjacent to the railway and their uses; for a layout based on modern-day practices, this can be accessed from photos, plans and even Google Streetview; for a layout based in a specific historical period, old photographs and maps will provide the best sources of information. Again, street names will give clues as to past land uses that may have been in place during the period planned for the layout. For example, Gasworks Street would indicate the presence of a once-common sight in towns in the nineteenth and early twentieth centuries – a lineside coal gasworks, an industrial activity from the steam age. Such clues to historical land

use will give the modeller ideas for his or her layout.

- The state of the vegetation – whether it has been maintained or left to overgrow some areas – can be important in setting the time period of a layout.
- Litter and rubbish dumped on or adjacent to railway land is a particularly unfortunate phenomenon of the mid- to late twentieth-century railway infrastructure, which can add realism to a layout.
- For modern image layouts, it is useful to look at how track layouts have been rationalized;

one idea is to model the space where there may have been track, but which has reverted to scrubland, or the land that may have been reclaimed from the railway for another use such as light industrial or even modern residential.

- Another particularly useful indicator in modern urban areas is the old railway company building that no longer forms part of the railway infrastructure; in many cases, the buildings and lands have been sold off and are now used for another purpose; this is particu-larly relevant to many station goods sheds and old engine sheds.

Fig. 16   Extensive stone retaining walls at Teignmouth Station show how the railway has a tightly constrained route in to the town and is typical of many urban railway scenes.

Fig. 17   A busy urban main-line station scene at Hamburg, Germany, with local commuter trains and high-speed ICE trains at the platforms.

If the proposed model railway is not based on a real location, but is intended as a fictional location in a specific area of the country, it might be helpful to think about the general geographical area and era in which the model is set. Is it a 1930s period layout set on the edge of a market town in the border counties of England and Scotland? Is it somewhere in rural mid-Wales in the late nineteenth century? Is it set in the flat, low-lying fens of Cambridgeshire and Norfolk during the late twentieth century? Such combinations of era and geographical area can provide some focus for the modeller in researching information for a layout, as well as giving good general indicators of land form, the land use in the period in question, and the extent of the railway infrastructure in that period.

The area and time period may be researched using railway company and general regional text books, internet and local resources for photographs, maps, drawings, land use listings, as well as any other information sources that are available. The key features that characterize an area are rock type, the shape of the landscape, industrial buildings, the style of the local buildings, and the colour of the local brick. Look at the railway companies that operated in that area to see how they approached the construction of the key elements of infrastructure.

DRAWING UP A PLAN

A plan for a layout is not essential, but it is a good idea to avoid wasting time and money on trying to build something that may ultimately either not work or meet the operating expectations. A layout plan will probably fall in to one of three categories:

1. A plan based on a real location and published railway company plan.
2. A plan based on no specific location, but containing features influenced by real locations, lineside industries, and railway company or regional practices.
3. A plan that is completely fictitious and freelance; this type of plan is typical of many narrow-gauge layouts.

Once you have a setting in mind for your model railway, you can plan out on paper, or electronically using one of the software packages available, to see how the layout might look and how the urban or rural landscape can be blended in to the layout. Planning using either method allows you to play around with combinations of track and scenery and move features around, without abortive construction work or the cost of wasted materials. Graph paper, a rule and a pencil are the basic layout tools, but an electronic package can offer some interesting possibilities. Whichever method you choose, the point is that you need to be able to change the plan as many times as necessary. The only real cost is your time, and it all adds to the fun of railway modelling.

When considering the third option – planning a layout that is not based on an actual location – it might be useful to list the key features that you would like to include. This list will be governed by personal preference and there is no specific right or wrong as to what features or operational requirements should be represented. Notwithstanding this, though, if you want your layout to be realistic in appearance, as well as representative of a particular railway company, period or region, the plan should recognize the style of railway infrastructure and the scenic setting typically associated with these criteria.

A MODEL RAILWAY IN THE LANDSCAPE

It is important to remember that in the real world the scenery or natural landscape was there long before the railways were even thought about as a method of transport, never mind actually planned and built. In order to make a model railway look more realistic, the aim ought to be, where reasonably practical, to make the track and infrastructure look like they have been built into the scenery or the landscape. It should not look like a flat baseboard with a track, with elements of scenery placed randomly on it as an afterthought and with no connection to each other or to the railway.

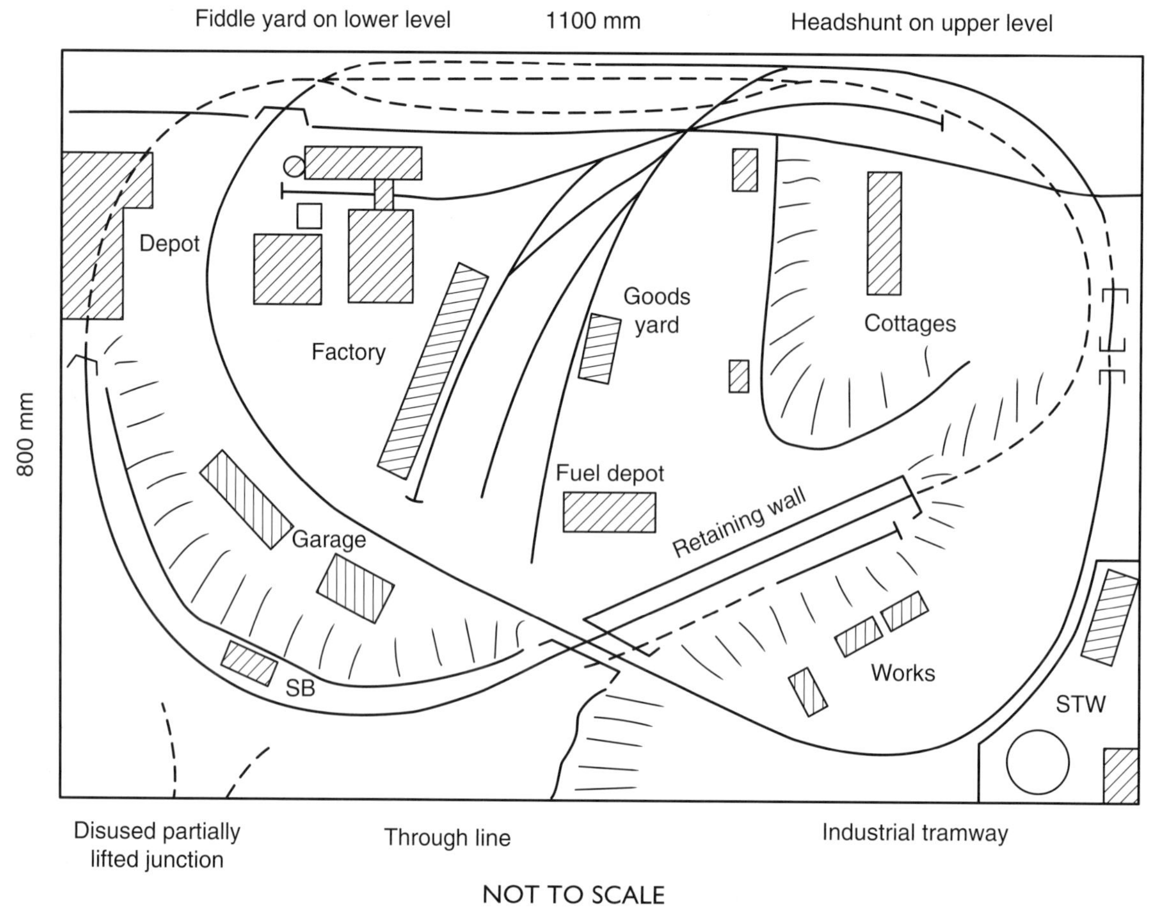

Fiddle yard on lower level   1100 mm   Headshunt on upper level

800 mm

Depot

Factory

Goods yard

Cottages

Fuel depot

Retaining wall

Garage

SB

Works

STW

Disused partially lifted junction

Through line

Industrial tramway

NOT TO SCALE

Fig. 18   Drawing up a sketch plan of the proposed layout allows the modeller to move and change features before committing to building anything – or spending any money! This example is my N-gauge layout 'Duddeston Junction'.

Fig. 19   The creation of a freelance narrow-gauge layout, such as my 'Gylchfan' OO9 micro-layout, allows the modeller to include a range of features that are not necessarily based on an actual location.

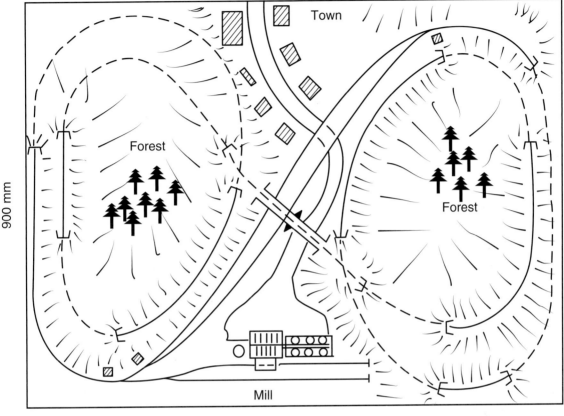

Fig. 20 *Using mapping-type symbols when sketching out a layout plan helps visualize how the 2-D plan will look as a 3-D model; this example is the N-gauge layout 'Pine Ridge Creek' built by Jersey Model Railway Club.*

Careful thought at the planning stage as to where the model railway layout is to be set, even as simple a distinction as to whether it is rural or urban, will allow the modeller to make some decisions about the landscape to model. For example, if the layout is to be set in a rural landscape with rolling hills, you will need to take into account the requirements for the gradients. The infrastructure for the railway should be designed to keep the track gradients as shallow as possible. Achieving this in a rolling hilly landscape will demand the use of cuttings or tunnels through hills, and embankments, bridges or viaducts over valleys and low-lying areas. In model form this means thinking about how the scenery will be developed above and below the level of the track bed.

In an urban setting, the railway was often threaded through areas of existing development. In model form this could involve extended embankments or cuttings through the urban area or long viaducts, with other land uses evident on the ground below the viaduct arches.

When planning layouts, it is a good idea to sketch ideas for the scenery at the same time as the track plan to see what might work and what might not. Using simple map symbols to show areas of raised topography will allow you to visualize what the completed model might look like. The same process can also be achieved with track-planning software, which creates a 3-D image of the intended layout on the screen.

Fig. 21   Constructing card mock-ups of key buildings is a quick and cheap way to work out sizes and layouts before scratch-building the final structures.

To provide emphasis to the 2-D drawing, it might be worth building mock-ups of structures and key features and putting them on the paper plan before cutting any wood or laying any track. When building an extension to my 'Llanfair & Meifod' layout, I used this method for the freight interchange section between the narrow-gauge and standard-gauge railway systems, which required the construction of a number of buildings bespoke to the location. My intention was that all the buildings would be either scratch-built or heavily modified kits, rather than ready-to-plant structures. Before starting any work on the buildings, mock-ups were created, to work out the exact size and shape that they would need to be. All the mock-ups were made from thick card, mostly recycled packaging, in true Blue Peter style,

with the plain card surface on the outer face of the buildings.

Creating a mock-up for the 'L'-shaped building was particularly useful in order to get the angles correct for the roof, which also had a truncated corner. It took several attempts cutting the card to get the right shape for the roof profile and to make it look correct. The card building was then disassembled and the card parts used as templates for marking on the embossed plasticard, which was used to form the walls and roof of the final structure.

The key advantage of mock-ups is that they allow you to play around with the shapes of the structures before deciding on the final layout and proceeding to the actual building. The only waste is the pieces of card, which can then go to be recycled.

Fig. 22   Finalizing the design of the scratch-built factory building on 'Llanfair & Meifod', with its complicated roof and angled wall that was needed to fit a restricted site on the layout, was made easier with the trial and error of the card mock-ups first.

BASEBOARD CONSTRUCTION

A key element in scenery planning for a model railway is to imagine the area being modelled or the general landscape characteristic features in a fictional setting and then decide how this can be accommodated at the baseboard construction stage. Thinking about the land above and below track-bed level will give a more realistic, rather than a 'flat-earth', appearance. It is definitely worth devoting time to the careful planning of a layout prior to construction, as this will all help with getting the landscape right in the final model.

Ron Pybus (2015) gives concise clear guidance on baseboard construction techniques. The following is a summary of the two main approaches: solid or open-frame. Each method has its merits and application and no one is better than the other. I have used both these techniques many times, often together in the same layout.

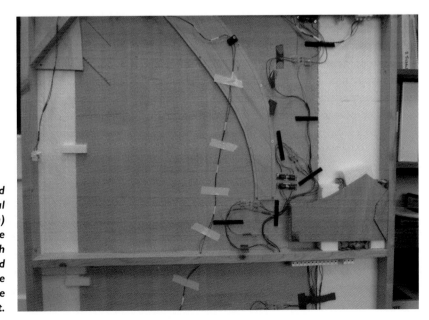

Fig. 23   A solid baseboard construction with typical 25 x 50mm (1 x 2in) planed softwood frame and a plywood top, with timber cross-bracing and polystyrene infill on the scenic margins of the baseboard to reduce weight.

SOLID BASEBOARD

A solid baseboard is the traditional method of construction and begins with the building of a frame, typically from softwood or plywood. Planed softwood timber 44 x 18mm (nominally 2 x 1in) is a commonly used material and the frame is constructed to the size of the planned baseboard, with suitable cross-bracing. Gluing and screwing all joints, using good-quality wood glue and 50–75mm wood screws, gives the best long-term joint construction and the strongest. Skimping on the quality of products at this stage will result in a baseboard that is highly likely to warp or to come apart with age.

With the frame built, a surface board is required. Various wood products can be used, with the choice often being down to personal preference. I like to use good-quality plywood of 6mm or 9mm thickness, although occasionally 12mm thickness is better for larger board areas to give added strength and rigidity. Plywood is relatively light and provides a strong base on which to build a layout.

Driving track pins into plywood can be difficult sometimes, depending on the thickness of any material (such as cork or polystyrene sheet) that may have been used below the track to deaden noise, or whether the track is fixed directly to the plywood surface. A thin layer of 2mm polystyrene sheet, supplied as a roll from most DIY stores, may be cut to shape for the track bed and then glued to the plywood with PVA-type adhesive. The track can then be glued in position on the polystyrene sheet with more PVA, with occasional pins used to hold it in position until the glue sets. After the ballast has been added as well, the track will be firmly fixed.

Other possible baseboard materials include the specialist board called Sundela, which makes a good solid base and provides an element of sound-deadening from the rolling stock running on the surface. This product does however require plenty of cross-bracing on the frame to prevent bowing of the surface over time and it can also be prone to expansion and warping if it gets damp. Where the location of the layout is prone to damp or a highly variable temperature range, use of this type of material needs to be carefully considered. Extra bracing and treatment of the baseboard, for example, sealing it with paint, will all help reduce the risk of deformation.

For a fixed layout, MDF or chipboard may be used as the surface board, although it should be noted that these two products are particularly heavy. Also, they are not really suitable for layouts that are subject to damp and cold conditions, as might be the case in a garden shed or garage, as this may result in warping of the boards. As with the Sundela board, the risk of this happening can be mitigated to a degree by additional bracing and by painting the baseboards to seal them before starting any layout construction.

Chipboard and MDF are also quite dense and heavy materials and may not be applicable for a layout designed to be transportable, unless you fancy a good workout each time the layout needs to be moved. At my local model railway club, many of the older layout baseboards were built using chipboard and substantial timber frames to prevent warping, and required a small army to move them. As that 'army' has grown older, a more lightweight baseboard philosophy has been adopted for any new layouts!

OPEN-FRAME BASEBOARD

The construction of an open-frame baseboard is similar to that of a solid one. Finalize the layout plan, deciding on the location of the track bed and the key landscape features to be included. Starting with softwood timber or plywood, you can then build a frame for the baseboard area. If there are to be significant level variations on the layout, the need for careful planning is emphasized, as this will affect the depth of the framing. If you are considering significant vertical differences in levels, plywood is likely to be more suitable than softwood to build the frame.

With the design decisions made, the frame can be built up following the same procedure as for the solid baseboard, using glue and screws for the joints. If you are considering using plywood to form the open-top framing, and you have reasonable carpentry skills, you can cut and slot the plywood frame and

Fig. 24 An open-frame baseboard, with the same timber framing and plywood track beds in the upper half and a solid section of board on the lower half.

cross-bracing pieces together. This will increase the rigidity and strength of the final structure. However, if your carpentry skills are less developed, you can use plywood with supporting softwood blocks at the joints if you are building a layout with a deeper plywood frame.

Once the frame has been built, the track bed, formed from your choice of base material, should be cut and fixed to the frame using supporting pieces of timber risers as required. This will allow the track beds to rise and/or fall within the framework for the creation of embankments. It is also useful at this stage to add additional formers fixed to the frame, to help with the creation of the layout scenery. These formers can be made from thin plywood and con-toured to match the proposed ground profile at the location on the layout.

In some circumstances, it may be appropriate to adopt both the open-top and the solid baseboard construction method on the same layout, depending on the setting being modelled, rather than doggedly sticking with one format.

BASEBOARD EXAMPLES

I have used both methods of baseboard construction on my layouts over the years, to replicate more real-istic scenery where required. For example, on the OO-gauge layout 'Llanfair & Meifod' (see Figure 24), using the open-top method enabled me to construct embankments to raise the standard-gauge running line over the narrow-gauge line at Meifod station. As well as achieving the necessary track-bed levels and adjacent realistic-looking landscape, one significant bonus of using the open-top method of baseboard construction was the reduction in both the weight of the baseboard and in the cost of the wood to build the basic shell.

I have also used solid baseboard construction for the main station areas on both OO-gauge and N-gauge layouts, where there was a concentration of track and where in reality it would have been a relatively flat area. However, even in the main branch station area on the OO-gauge layout 'Llanfair & Meifod', I included a slight rise in the track bed from the main running line to the engine shed facility, just to give a bit more perspective to the layout and to give the impression of the railway infrastructure adapting to the landscape. At this location on the layout I was then able to add a locomotive service pit as part of the shed facility, set into the raised ground level and with a hole cut into the plywood baseboard surface.

Fig. 25 Meifod interchange station for the narrow- and standard-gauge lines on my 'Llanfair & Meifod' OO-gauge layout was built utilizing open-frame baseboard techniques.

LAYING THE TRACK

Once the baseboard has been constructed, the next stage is to lay the track – the part that most railway modellers really look forward to. After all the doodling and drawing of track plans, and creating the baseboard, it is now time to move beyond the armchair planning stage and actually lay something on which to run the rolling stock. Before you get too carried away, though, there are a few things to bear in mind when putting down the track.

The track will need to be supported on a track bed and little issues such as gradients, tolerances and clearances need to be considered before you rashly cover your baseboard with scale miles of track. The following advice is not intended to curb your enthusiasm for track laying, but to help you avoid wasted effort and costs, as well as potential frustration later when your prized rolling stock will not negotiate the track plan of your too hastily laid layout.

Fig. 26 Construction of the engine shed facility on a solid baseboard, using polystyrene sheeting to create a ground profile.

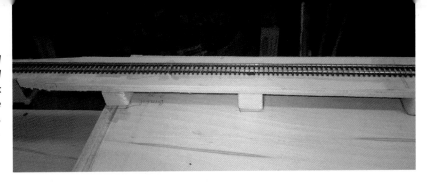

Fig. 27   Raised track bed supported on softwood timber off-cuts, with track laid and ready to form the embankment slopes.

THE TRACK BED

Where open-top baseboard construction methods have been used, the track bed can be formed from thin plywood sheets or more substantial timber, depending on the scale and number of tracks being constructed. For OO-gauge and N-gauge layouts, 4mm thickness plywood should suffice for the track bed, coupled with plenty of timber supports to the frame of the baseboard. To ensure that the track bed does not warp, the support timbers should be spaced no more than about 150mm to 200mm apart. (This is not a precise measurement and is largely based on your experience of layout construction and the size and shape of the layout under construction.)

When preparing the board used for the track bed, it is important to ensure that it is wide enough to accommodate the running line or lines, with the appropriate scale clearances between and adjacent to these running lines. The track-bed board should also be wide enough to provide support for the immediate area to the side of the tracks, to accommodate ballast shoulders and, if necessary, any lineside building or equipment, although this last part is not essential.

There is no fixed rule for this, but by way of guidance when planning your track bed, the track-bed board required for an OO-gauge single track should be at least 50mm wide. For an N-gauge single line, the track-bed board should be at least 30mm wide. Another consideration when deciding on the width of your track bed boards is that, if there is sufficient space, the width of board could also allow the blending of the adjacent landscape in the open-top sections of the baseboard into the track bed in a realistic manner, without any abrupt and unrealistic changes in ground profile.

Notwithstanding these remarks, in certain circumstances the width of the track-bed board may be narrower to reflect a particular landscape scenario being modelled. As an example, the N-gauge club layout 'Pine Ridge Creek', constructed by the N-gauge section of the Jersey Model Railway Club, was based on North American prototype practice. On this particular layout the track bed was modelled

Fig. 28   The N-gauge 'Pine Ridge Creek' layout by the Jersey Model Railway Club – a North American-themed layout with track bed spiralling up from the central section on to 'ledges' in the mountainous scenery.

Fig. 29 OO-gauge Code 100 track laid on a 2mm polystyrene sheet and then carefully painted and ballasted gives a realistic track bed.

to represent a line winding through mountainous scenery on ledges blasted into the mountain side.

With this concept in mind, the track-bed boards on the layout were planned to be located in places that were narrower than the generally recommended dimensions. This allowed for the replication of steep rock faces above and below the track-bed level with minimum loading gauge clearances, to try and get the feel of the prototype. Judging by the comments received from some of the visitors to the club's annual exhibition, including several from the USA and Canada, the overall effect was achieved!

On a solid baseboard surface there is less of a requirement for a raised track bed, but there may be a need to raise the track above the level of the main baseboard surface. This can be simply achieved using a thin layer of cork sheeting (approximately 2mm thick for OO-gauge). This has the effect of raising the track slightly so that when it is ballasted you get the shoulders of the ballast at the edges of the track bed, as well as providing a material that will help deaden any sound of the rolling stock running across a plywood surface.

A number of suppliers provide ready-made cork or polystyrene sheeting cut to size for the standard track gauges. A cheaper alternative is to use cork sheets or rolls of polystyrene sheeting from the local DIY store and cut them to fit your particular track layout.

Fig. 30 Cork tiles or rolls of polystyrene sheet available from most good DIY stores can provide effective material for track on a layout, and may be cheaper than some of the products marketed specifically towards the railway modeller.

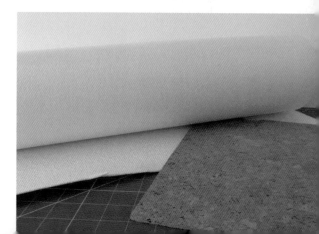

GRADIENTS

The gradients of real railways were designed to be as shallow as possible, but this is less practicable in model form, unless space is not an issue. Keeping to the recommended track gradients as used in the real world would necessitate large areas of construction, so the modeller will almost always have to make compromises between realism and what it is possible to build in the space or baseboard size available.

In order to keep the gradients as realistic as possible in a model layout, it is sometimes useful and/ or necessary to use scenery to disguise significant gradient rises and make them look more realistic. For standard-gauge lines, tunnels and hidden track sections behind scenery can be used to raise or lower track-bed levels. On the N-gauge layout 'Pine Ridge Creek', tunnels were used to disguise spiral embankments with steeper gradients in the tunnelled sections and slacker gradients on the viewable sections, creating a scene that is more believable overall.

For narrow-gauge layouts, gradient tolerances are more severe in the real world. Therefore, in model form steeper gradients do not necessarily look out of place, as long as they are modelled carefully and are constructed within the traction limits of the

Fig. 31   Spiral track beds in tunnels on an N-gauge layout create more running length in a smaller area. The spirals are partially hidden in the scenery.

model locomotives intended to negotiate them. For some simple tests that can be used to find the optimum gradient for your rolling stock on a layout, *see* Chapter 4.

Where one track crosses over or under another, requiring track gradients to the crossing bridge, one useful trick in the real world is to lower one line slightly, whilst at the same time raising the other to achieve the bridge clearances at the cross-over point. This can also work in model railway construction, effectively halving the distance required to obtain the track clearance above the lower track (see Chapter 4). If done carefully, with good scenic modelling, it can look convincingly realistic.

On my OO-gauge 'Llanfair & Meifod' layout I employed this technique using an open baseboard construction method. The standard-gauge line needed to be raised by at least 45mm to achieve the minimum clearance for the narrow-gauge rolling stock at the over-bridge, which crossed the narrow-gauge line at the Meifod station interchange. In addition to this vertical constraint, the starting point and end point of the standard-gauge line at the baseboard joints needed to be uniform, to fit with the remainder of the layout sections.

The layout is of modular construction, so that it can be rearranged in a number of different baseboard configurations to fit the space available. To achieve this flexibility in baseboard configuration, the baseboard joint and track location points are common on a number of board modules, providing a horizontal constraint to the embankment construction. Both the vertical and horizontal constraints also had to be accommodated on a curved track section on the standard gauge – just to complicate matters further.

To achieve the cross-over without steep, non-prototypical-looking gradients on either the main or narrow-gauge line, each line was constructed on its own track bed. The track bed for the narrow-gauge line was fixed to the open frame so that it descended approximately 25mm either side of the over-bridge, whilst the track bed for the standard-gauge line was fixed on formers so that is rose approximately 20mm from the baseboard joints to either side of the over-bridge. The landscape in between the track

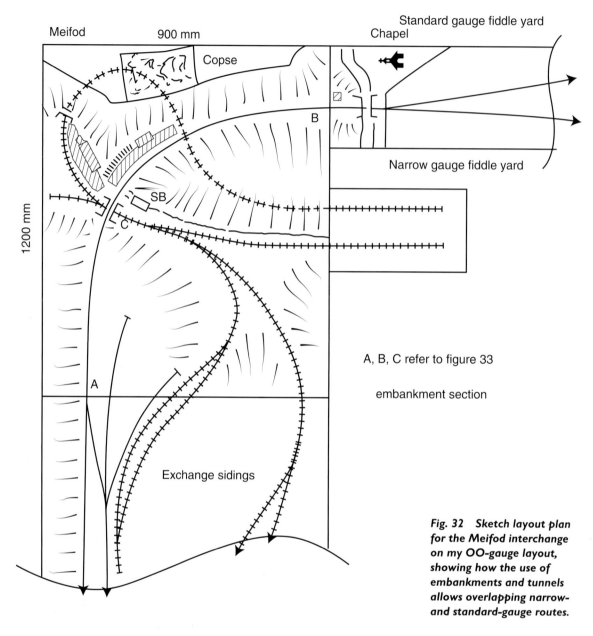

Fig. 32 Sketch layout plan for the Meifod interchange on my OO-gauge layout, showing how the use of embankments and tunnels allows overlapping narrow- and standard-gauge routes.

beds was then added and modelled to create an effective – and hopefully realistic-looking – scene of the railway in the landscape.

TOLERANCES AND CLEARANCES

The issue of tolerances and clearances is a key consideration during baseboard construction and layout planning, in particular when it comes to thinking about the scenery to be modelled. The use of track

templates, such as those from Peco Streamline, when drawing on paper or creating a plan using software will help with checking clearances between tracks, and with cuttings, embankments, bridges and general landscape scenery.

The next step is to look at the rolling stock that you expect to run on the layout and check the dimensions of the largest locomotive and piece of bogie rolling stock, if appropriate. Taking the loco

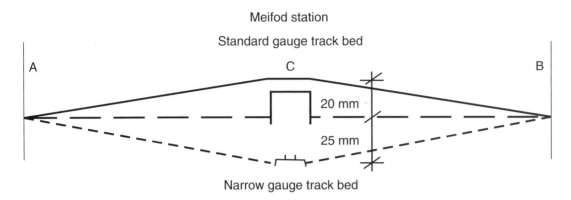

Meifod station

Standard gauge track bed

A   C   B

20 mm

25 mm

Narrow gauge track bed

Fig. 33   Cross-section of the standard-gauge route through the station, showing the rising standard-gauge line and the lowered narrow-gauge line, achieving the height required for the cross-over point of the two lines.

Fig. 34   The standard-gauge line crossing the narrow-gauge line at Meifod station.

and rolling stock, trace the clearances required on curves using a pencil held beside the item of rolling stock as required through curves, point-work, and so on, especially where you have more than one track running parallel.

For the rolling stock, it is advisable to take your longest bogie coach or wagon, then use a pencil held at the mid-point to mark the inside of curves for clearance (*see* Figure 35). Similarly, hold a pencil at the outer end corner of the vehicle to trace the arc traversed by the vehicle along the outside of a curve. The area between the two lines gives the minimum clearance requirement for your rolling stock on that running line.

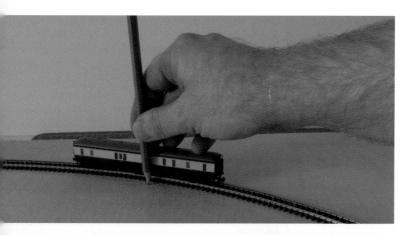

Fig. 35 Marking the track clearance on the inside of a curve using the centre point of a bogie coach.

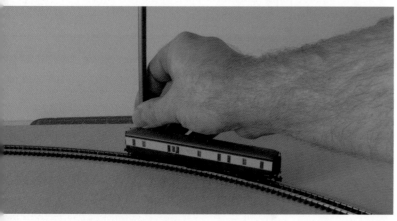

Fig. 36 Marking the track clearance on the outside of a curve using the outside leading corner of a bogie coach.

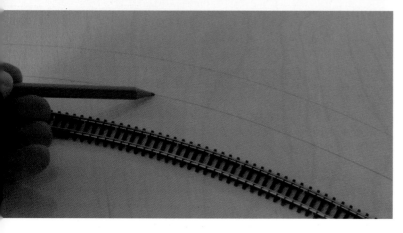

Fig. 37 The two marked lines provide the clearance required for rolling stock through the curved track section.

To check the clearances for your locomotives through bridges, tunnels and, importantly, station platforms, measure the width of each of your locomotives, including, where present, any outside cylinders for steam locos. As with the rolling stock, you can use a pencil held at the widest point of the loco to trace the clearance along each side of the track. Alternatively, it might help to mock up a card gauge for the height and width of the rolling stock and use it for checking around the proposed layout.

Fig. 38 *Tracing the clearance required for outside cylinder steam locomotives on the inside of a curve.*

Fig. 39 *A simple height gauge cut from 2mm artist's card provides a quick and cheap method of checking clearances for bridges, tunnels, station canopies, and so on.*

In urban settings in the real world, where there would have been many competing uses for the limited land available and land costs would have been at a premium, railways were often squeezed into tight close-tolerance spaces or routes, with minimum clearances for rolling stock. Some railway routes even had restrictions and bespoke-designed and built rolling stock to fit within very tight loading gauge parameters. Research of the prototype on which the layout is to be modelled will assist in identifying these types of requirements. In model form, minimum clearances can help with squeezing track formations into small spaces on a baseboard, in order to achieve a realistic-looking layout. The concept is often used in mini- or micro-layout construction.

ACCEPTING COMPROMISE

From time to time, the modeller needs to accept some compromises in layout construction where layout space and/or baseboard sizes are restricted. Realistic embankment gradients can be achieved using modelling techniques to hide or disguise non-prototypical track-bed rises. Elsewhere, careful positioning of tunnels can be used to disguise steeper gradients of the track bed (*see* Chapter 3), as well as non-prototypical sharp corners in a track layout.

CHAPTER THREE

CREATING TUNNELS

In essence, tunnels were built on full-sized railways by engineers trying to find a way through the landscape, where it was not practical or possible to deviate around a natural obstruction or a human settlement. The choice as to whether to proceed with excavating a cutting or a tunnel was largely governed by the cost and the geology along the route of the proposed railway line.

Generally, a tunnel is more expensive to construct when compared with the cost of digging a cutting, but in some rock types the amount of land needed to form a cutting with long-term, stable sides will be significant. As a result, depending on track-bed level and the depth of cutting required, tunnelling is sometimes the better option in terms of cost and engineering.

USING TUNNELS ON A LAYOUT

ADDING REALISM

Tunnels have a number of uses on model railway layouts. First, they add a third dimension – namely height – by creating a landscape above track level that can be used to model rural or urban scenes.

A tunnel on a layout should be planned to ensure that it appears realistic and reflects a railway in the landscape; it should not look like an unnatural mound on a flat baseboard surface. If it is successful, this is the sort of feature that distinguishes a first train set from a model railway. A rolling landscape or a series of gorges and mountain slopes will provide dramatic scenery for the layout and allow the inclusion of

Fig. 40 A local train entering one of the tunnels on the route west of Dawlish, UK; the extra supporting arch and brick retaining wall to the right support the hillside above.

Fig. 41 A tunnel entrance taking the track through the mountainous scenery on an N-gauge North American-themed layout.

tunnels and other pieces of railway infrastructure, such as bridges, viaducts, cuttings and embankments. All these features will make a model railway appear much more realistic. Michael Andress, in his *PSL Model Railway Guide 2 – Layout Planning* (1981) also makes the point that, for a tunnel on a layout to appear convincing, the hill through which the railway passes must be high enough and wide enough so that it would not have been possible or practical to carry the railway around it or through a cutting.

SCENIC BREAKS

Tunnels are commonly used on a model railway layout as a scenic break, typically to hide the access to a fiddle yard, or to provide a break between different scenic sections of a layout. Often a tunnel on a layout will be used to disguise a sharp or non-prototypical turn in the track between scenic sections of a layout, at the entrance to a fiddle yard or to negotiate a curve within the physical limits of the baseboard or modelling area available. In these cases, the tunnel can be used to suggest an extension of the layout or modelled scene beyond the physical layout limit. In

a rural setting, this may be accomplished by blending the ground modelled above the tunnel into the back scene to give the impression of hills or mountains into the distance.

In a more urban setting, the ground above the tunnel could contain buildings in full or partial relief in front of a back scene that has an urban landscape applied, as on my N-gauge layout 'Duddeston Junction' (see later).

Careful planning of tunnel locations can allow the railway modeller to break up a layout into a number of distinct scenic sections, to make the best use of limited modelling space. For example, a country branch-line station could be modelled in one section, then a tunnel scenic break could be used to suggest the continuation of the running line to the next section, which might be another station, industrial site, or urban setting. The options are limited only by the imagination of the modeller constructing the layout, but the key point is that the tunnel in this instance is used to disguise the proximity of different scenic sections so as to make the most of the modelling area.

Fig. 42 The exit from the fiddle yard on my OO9 micro-layout is disguised as a tunnel through an industrial site.

Fig. 43 In a rural setting, the tunnel and hillside on Pete Waterman's O-gauge 'Leamington Spa' layout blend into the back scene, creating a realistic model.

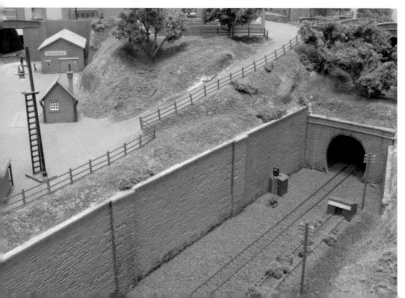

Fig. 44 The retaining walls and tunnel on my N-gauge layout 'Duddeston Junction' help create a strong sense of the urban theme.

CHANGING GRADIENTS

Tunnelled sections may also be used on a layout to disguise changes of gradient that may not be proto-typical but are made necessary by the restrictions of the space available. This can allow steeper straight section climbs between different levels of a layout or, in more elaborate set-ups, spiral track beds can be hidden in tunnels to disguise level and gradient changes. The example described later was con-structed for an N-gauge layout, but the principles are the same for other gauges and scales.

DISGUISING CONTINUOUS-RUN LAYOUTS

The use of tunnels on a tail chaser-type layout allows it to be broken down into a number of discrete sec-tions or scenes, which can be used to create the impression of a model railway in the landscape rather than just a train set. This approach was used on my N-gauge layout 'Duddeston Junction' (see later). Tunnelled sections can also be created to hide additional storage tracks for trains, as well as to dis-guise return loops on a single track layout, creating the impression that the tracks extend further than they actually do.

The use of return loops needs to be carefully considered on a single-track layout. There will be a requirement to create an electrical break in the loop to change the polarity on the return, in order to prevent a short circuit. Reference to guidance on track electrification and polarity in respect of return loops, such as that given in Michael Andress's *PSL Model Railway Guide 1*, is recommended reading for anyone considering the use of a return loop.

CONSTRUCTING TUNNELS

The following methods and techniques for creating tunnels for a model railway layout have been used on a number of different layouts in various scales. It is not intended to be an exhaustive digest on tunnel building – there are many ways in which tunnels can be constructed – but it does aim to give guidance on how I created the tunnels on the various layouts that I have constructed over the years.

PORTALS AND WING WALLS

The construction of a tunnel will start with the portal and wing walls, the most visible part of the feature. In model form, portals and wing walls can be fabricated from kits; they may be represented by ready-to-plant structures, which are supplied by a number of manu-facturers; or they can be scratch-built using a wide range of materials.

Kits for tunnel portals are available in many scales and in different types of material. The most commonly used are plastic, paper/card or plaster mouldings, but it is also possible to buy kits in resin and wood. Making tunnel portals from kits is a good way to make a realistic structure for a layout. When moving on to scratch-building, it is important to get the proportions correct, and building kits can help with future layout construction. They certainly offer a good starting point.

Plastic Kits

Plastic kits, such as those produced by Peco in N-, OO- and O-gauge, are the most common types of kit. They are ready-coloured and can be used straight from the pack if desired, although a little attention in terms of painting and subtle weathering can enhance the appearance and give a more realistic result. The kits comprise the portal wall and two wing walls in O- and OO-gauge, whilst in N-gauge two portals and four wing walls are provided. The pieces are well moulded and make a good representation of a stone tunnel portal and wing wall arrangement.

For a brick tunnel portal, the OO-gauge plastic kit available from Wills is a good example. This type of kit is more complicated than the Peco ones, requiring an element of cutting and fixing together sections of embossed brick plasticard sheets, to create the portal and wing walls, before painting to produce a finished model. The advantage over the ready-formed portals is the ability to adjust the kit components to meet specific requirements on a par-ticular layout.

The Wills kit has very few component parts. The brief instructions are provided on a single sheet of A5, with an exploded image of the kit parts showing their relative position to each other in the completed

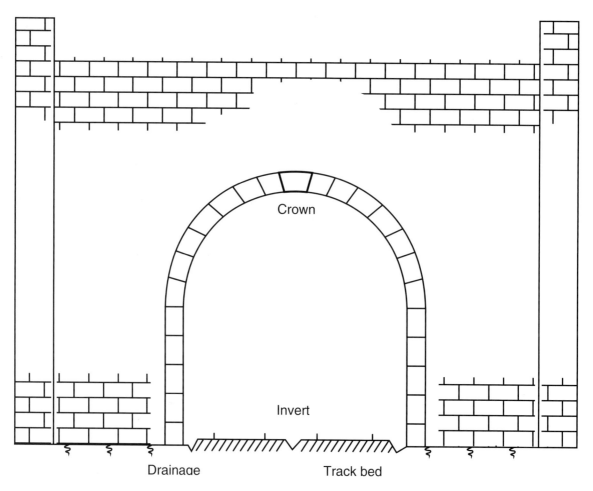

Fig. 45   Sketch of a typical tunnel portal to help identify the key structural elements.

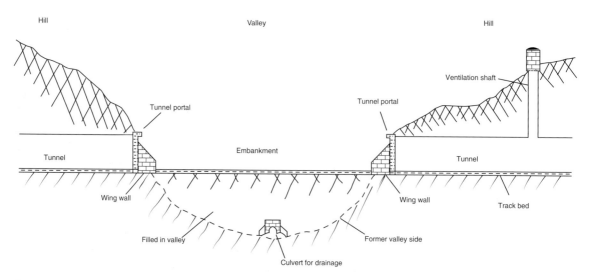

Fig. 46   Sketch cross-section through a typical tunnel to indicate common features associated with these important elements of railway infrastructure.

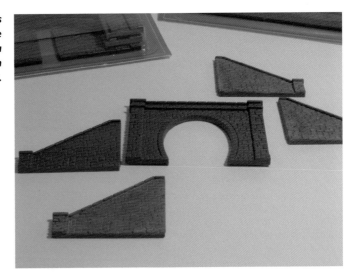

Fig. 47 Moulded plastic tunnel portals and wing walls such as these, which are available from Peco in N-gauge, provide a good starting point for creating a tunnel on a layout.

Fig. 48 The embossed plasticard kit of a brick tunnel portal can be relatively quickly made up in to a realistic piece of railway infrastructure.

model. It is a simple kit to complete, but produces a realistic-looking and well-detailed brick tunnel portal. As with any plastic kit, the small parts should be carefully removed from the sprues to prevent damage to the embossed surface. The modeller has the option to paint before or after completion of the kit, but completing this type of kit first and then painting after makes it easier to hide any adhesive that may have leaked at the joints during construction.

The construction of the kit can be broken down in to four steps. The parapet wall for the top of the structure is fixed together using liquid polystyrene cement. While this is drying, a similar process is used for the buttresses at the ends of the wing walls. With these sub-assemblies finished and set, the structure can then be assembled either as a standalone structure to be placed on the baseboard at a later date, or built up in situ.

Start with the main portal wall and ensure that it is vertical in position on the baseboard or on the work bench before attaching the wing walls. Stand the wall against a metal right-angle while the wing walls are fixed in place. Once the wing walls have set, the structure is sell-supporting and the buttresses for the ends of each wing wall may

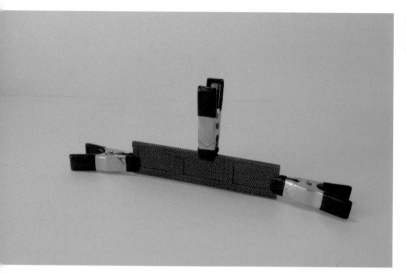

Fig. 49   The parapet wall is formed from two sections glued back to back to provide a scale thickness brick parapet structure.

Fig. 50   Ensuring the portal wall section is vertical before fixing the wing walls, utilizing a small engineer's square.

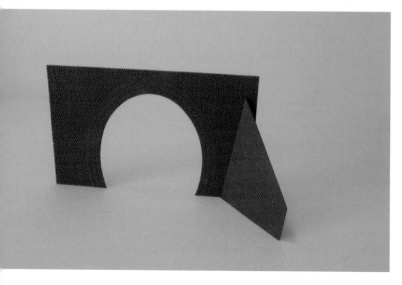

Fig. 51   The wing walls are fixed to the portal to match the location on the layout.

Fig. 52   With both wing walls in place the end buttresses are added. The final addition is the parapet wall.

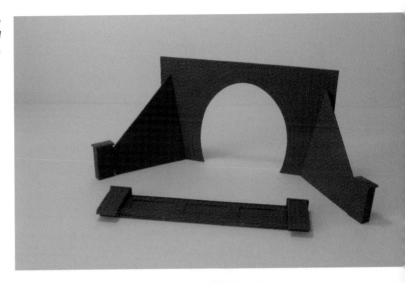

Fig. 53   The parapet is fixed to the top edge of the portal wall section.

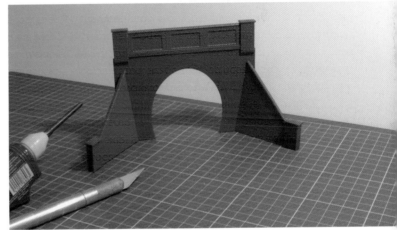

be added, followed last by the parapet wall sub-assembly.

The strength of the joint between the parapet wall sub-assembly and the main tunnel portal wall may be strengthened by using some scrap pieces of 2mm thick plasticard, in this case scraps of the embossed stone wall sheets from the Wills range. These pieces are glued to the rear face of the tunnel portal, flush with the top edge, and the parapet fixed on top. The joints between the wing walls and the front face of the portal wall are also strengthened, this time using off-cuts from the sprues in the kit.

Construction of the kit is possible within a single short modelling session. The painting of the completed structure can be left for another session.

Card Kits

Card kits are also quite common, with some of the best-known being produced by Superquick and Metcalfe Models. These kits can be made up relatively quickly and provide sturdy models of tunnel portals and associated structures, as well as the internal walls of the tunnel.

The Superquick kit (catalogue number A14) is marketed as a tunnel or road bridge kit, increasing its flexibility as a scenic break or as a free-standing structure on a layout. The Metcalfe kit (catalogue number PO243) is the OO-gauge model, but similar kits for N-gauge are also available from the same manufacturer. This kit includes plenty of spare parts for customization as well as the substantial card

Fig. 54 Scrap plasticard on the rear face of the portal wall, shown brown here, helps support the parapet wall.

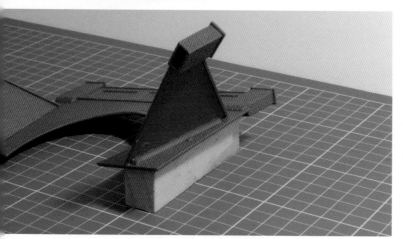

Fig. 55 To reinforce the joint between the wing wall and the portal wall, sections of the sprue to which the parts were moulded are cut and glued into the joint with liquid polystyrene cement.

Fig. 56 Check for track clearance before finally fixing to the baseboard; small wooden blocks provide additional support to the portal and fixing points to the baseboard.

Fig. 57 Detailed tunnel portal kits in card are available from a number of suppliers, including Metcalfe Kits and Superquick Model Kits.

structure to support the portal wall and tunnel lining. Good, effective and realistic tunnel mouths can be created in OO-gauge from card kits such as those produced by Metcalfe and Superquick.

A description of the construction of both of these types of kit follows, with notes that are intended to be complementary to the comprehensive instruction sheets provided with them. Before starting work, make sure that you have the right tools to hand, as well as an appropriate adhesive.

The Metcalfe kit (ref: PO243) represents a stone portal for a single track; similar kits are produced for double track in OO-gauge and also N-gauge. The tunnel portal kits follow the standard heavy-duty card format as used for the building range. Pack PO243 contains sufficient parts to create two single-track stone tunnel portals with wing walls and side walls, to be configured as required to suit a particular location.

As with all of these types of kit, read through the sheet of clear step-by-step guide instructions first and familiarize yourself with how the kit is intended to be put together. Look over the sheets of parts and check that they are all present and that you

Fig. 58 A selection of tools and adhesives is required for putting together the card kits, including white glue, impact adhesive, heavy-duty craft knife, fine detail knife and a sturdy pair of scissors.

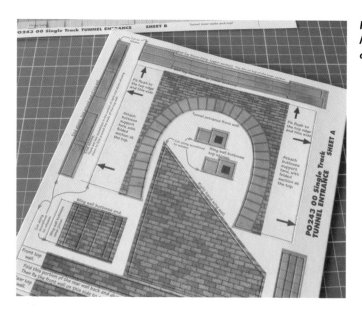

Fig. 59   The stone tunnel portal kit from Metcalfe is created from die-cut card, with a plethora of detail parts.

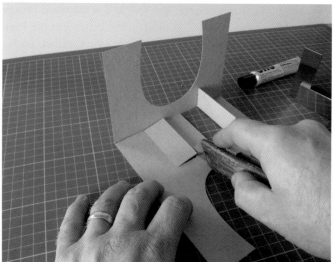

Fig. 60   A plain heavy-duty card structure forms the skeleton of the kit around which the printed parts are fixed.

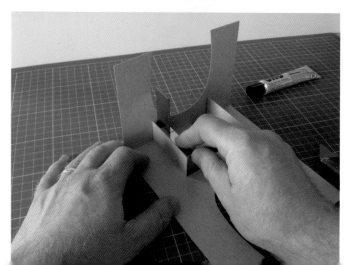

Fig. 61   Cutting and folding of the marked tabs to form the supporting frame.

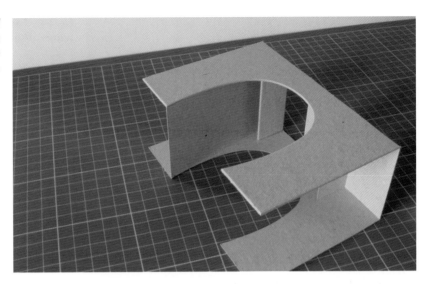

Fig. 62 The completed support structure with inclined internal bracing to accommodate the lining.

can identify them before cutting any parts from the sheets. This kit comprises two sheets of heavy-duty plain grey card formers and two sheets of printed parts for each tunnel portal.

Starting with the plain grey card sheet referred to as Sheet 1, the basic former for the kit is cut from the tabs and then folded up to make the support structure. When folded up and checked for alignment the joints should be glued with an impact adhesive such as UHU and left to set.

From Sheet 2 of the plain grey card, take the two rectangular pieces, which are additional support pieces that fit within the frame structure that you have created from Sheet 1, as explained in the instructions. Fit flush with the base of the structure as described, but make sure the part is angled to ensure that it does not impinge on the elliptical profile of the tunnel. It is also important to realize that when fitted flush, as described, with the base of the structure, the support sheet will not extend

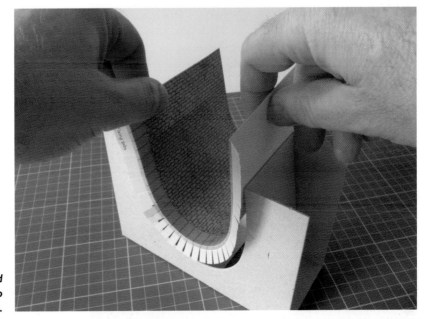

Fig. 63 Inserting the printed thin card lining sheet into the support frame.

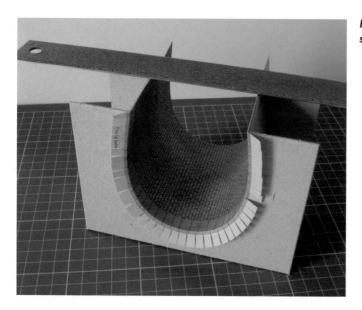

Fig. 64   Checking that the lining detail is square with the base of the structure.

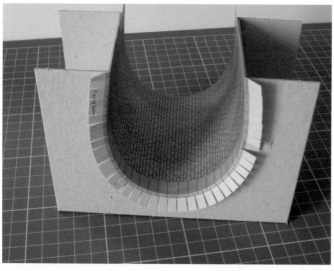

Fig. 65   The tabs are pre-cut and require bending and scoring at right angles to the back of the lining sheet; the tabs are then glued in place on the front wall of the frame.

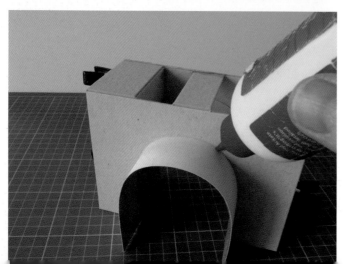

Fig. 66   White glue around the frame helps hold the lining paper firmly in place.

all the way to the top; you should expect to have a 2–3mm gap at the top.

When the card support structure is complete, the next stage is to insert the tunnel lining, which is provided as a pre-printed sheet on thick paper/thin card. This part is gently squeezed into the former that you have created and is held in place by gluing along the base and around the arch to fix the tabs, as shown in the instructions. Taking your time at this stage will pay off in the long run, resulting in a very neat finished model. This part is then set aside while the portal wall is built up.

Moving on to the sheet of printed parts, the first step is to cut the tabs to release the portal wall and then to add the buttress supports to the front of the portal wall on the sheet of pre-printed parts. When secure and square, the portal wall is fixed to the grey card former, over the tabs of the tunnel lining sheet, with the stone joints of the printed parts being lined up carefully. Small clips and pegs can be used to hold the portal section firmly in place on the former, until the adhesive sets, to ensure that there are no gaps around the edge of the kit.

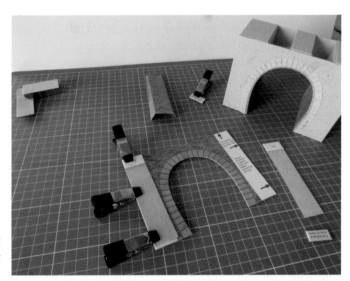

Fig. 67   The printed sheet tabs are folded up and left to dry with clips before moving to the next stage.

Fig. 68   The front portal wall is fixed to the frame and held in place until the glue has set.

Once the support structure has been set in place, the buttresses are folded up and added to the structure. Hold each part in place, pressing firmly along the joints with a piece of timber off-cut, until the adhesive has set. The instruction sheet is very clear about the need to make sure that the buttresses are fixed the correct way round, as they have a longer section on the outer edge. This longer part is designed to wrap over the outer edge of the portal wall, to hide the joint between the printed sheet and the grey card support structure.

While the portal section is hardening off, the parapet wall that extends across the top of the structure can be made up. It comprises a number of printed sections and the modeller needs to check that it is square and that the overhang of the capping stone section is uniform. When it is set, the wall is fixed across the top of the portal wall section, overhanging the front of the kit. The exact dimensions of the overhang are up to the model maker. I chose a 2–3mm overlap at the front and set back on to the top of the former. At this stage, some of the left-over grey card pieces may be used to form additional strengthening strips across the top of the structure. This also provides additional card on which to build off the overlying scenery.

The next step is to fix the side wall sections to the main structure. These can be as short or as long as you wish, to suit the location on your layout. The parts may even be omitted if not required. To fit the side walls as shown in the instructions, 3–4mm need to be trimmed from the top edge of the parts, to ensure that they fit under the top parapet wall/slab structure. It is also helpful to add further pieces of the heavy-duty grey card, made from off-cuts, to strengthen the join to the main support structure.

The last major step is to add the wing walls. These are built up as shown in the instructions, together with the short buttress columns, before fixing to the front of the tunnel portal. To improve the strength of the joint between the wing wall and the portal wall section, mark out on some scrap grey card the shape of the wedge between the rear face of the wing wall part and the front of the tunnel portal, then cut it to fit and glue it in place flush with the bottom edge of both parts. Adding this wedge part stops the wing wall 'flapping' about and makes the structure sturdier.

Once the wing walls have been fixed in place, the small buttress columns are added to the outer edge of the wing wall. The angle of the wing walls can be adjusted with minor trimming if necessary, to suit your layout requirements or, in some cases, omitted completely.

The finishing touches to the kit are the addition of the capping stones to the top of both the wing walls and side walls. Plenty of strips of capping stones are supplied with the kit in case you want more – or

Fig. 69 Check to ensure that the printed buttress sections are square before fixing permanently to the structure.

Fig. 70   The completed structure, minus wing walls, ready to put on the layout.

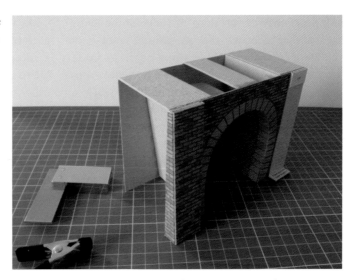

make a mess of your first attempts at cutting and fixing them in place! One strip cut exactly in half should be sufficient to cover both of the side walls. Each wing wall requires one strip to complete. To get an accurate length, use the cut-out on the main pre-printed sheet of parts as a guide to mark the strip, then use scissors to trim the upper end of each one where it abuts the portal wall, to get the correct angle and flush fit. This exact cut depends on the angle at which you have set the wall. This is best done after fixing the wall in place, trimming a bit at a time and test fitting until you are satisfied with the fit of the capping stones.

The kit is now finished, according to the instruction sheet, but it can be further enhanced. One perceived disadvantage of these kits is that the printed card components lack the depth of detail relief that is provided by kits constructed from plasticard or moulded in resin or plaster. However, depending on the kit's proposed location on the layout, and the scale being modelled, this may or may not be a significant issue. In my experience, when viewed from normal viewing distances, card kits in N-gauge are just as convincing as plastic kits.

To remove any signs of the underlying card – at the joints around the tunnel portal, for example – a

Fig. 71   Test-fitting the tunnel portal to check track clearances before finally fixing to the baseboard.

soft pencil may be run along the edge of the joints to shade it to match the pre-printed colours of the kit. It is also possible to use a pencil to shade around the top of the arch to help provide a representation of soot staining on the block work; a similar effect can also be achieved by dry brushing with acrylic paints.

The printed sheets of the kits can also be enhanced, with some subtle weathering and appropriately coloured paint around the exposed joints to hide the underlying white card. Using quick-drying acrylic paints will reduce the risk of damage to the card structure. Layers of paint may be built up for weathering and additional detailing in relatively quick succession and a good effect can usually be accomplished within a single modelling session.

At the bottom edge of the walls on the tunnel portal and wing walls, a selection of acrylic paint colours, with different shades of green, brown, yellow/ochre, black and possibly some reds/blues, may be dry brushed on to provide a realistic impression of weeds, moss and undergrowth at the base of the wall. This painting, combined with the effective use of ground cover scenic materials such as the products from Woodland Scenics, all helps produce a more realistic appearance to the structure set. (For more on weathering and use of ground cover scenic materials to blend structures into a landscape, see Chapter 7.)

As well as using paints to enhance the appearance of the card kit and to hide the exposed white card backing to the printed sheets, it is also possible to utilize detail parts made from plastic or some other material. For example, the addition of plastic moulded drainpipes, or stone detail for the portal, will give added relief to the structure.

One alternative to Metcalfe's stone portal kit is Superquick's red brick structure. Marketed as a bridge or tunnel, it contains parts that can be used to create either, but not both at the same time. As with the Metcalfe kit, there are printed sheets of card of varying thicknesses comprising die-cut parts to make up the kit.

The look of the kit is perhaps more appropriate for an urban layout. As produced, it has a tunnel mouth that is wide enough to accommodate double track, subject to checking clearances on your rolling stock and its intended location on the layout. As supplied, the kit builds up to form a portal wall with extended side walls beyond the buttresses. However, with careful cutting the kit could be modified so that the portal has wing walls, similar to the style adopted for the Metcalfe kit.

Construction of the Superquick kit requires more care and attention when cutting the parts from the pre-printed sheets. Many of the parts are interlocking on the sheet, so there is a risk of damaging them during the cutting-out stage. In addition, the tabs

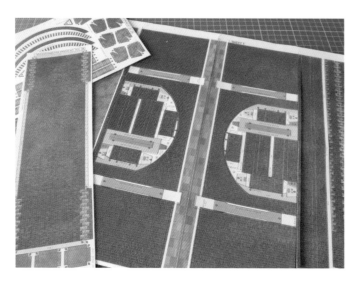

Fig. 72 A Superquick Models brick tunnel kit that can also be used as bridge sides, as detailed in the instruction sheet.

Fig. 73   The Superquick kit has more of
the parts interlocking on the base sheet,
requiring careful cutting when removing
them.

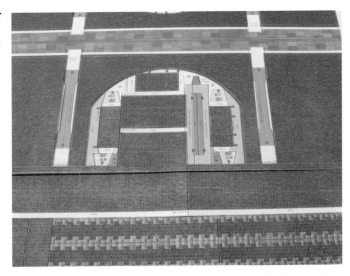

tend to be less obvious than on the Metcalfe kit, due to that close proximity of the parts.

Because of the way the kit is designed, with overlying parts, the gluing and folding of the tabs must be carried out one part at a time and left to harden off before continuing to the next stage of the kit construction. For example, the folding and sticking of the column caps and the wall sections folded around the former pieces of card needs to be done one side at a time, allowing the glue to harden off on one side before folding and gluing the next side. Putting together the kit is therefore a little fiddlier that the Metcalfe kit, but patience and slow progress

are rewarded with a good detailed model of a brick tunnel portal structure.

There is less of a supporting structure with this kit than the Metcalfe kit. It is left to the modeller to provide a portal support that is suitable for the location on his or her intended layout. It is a good idea to keep spare card from other kits for this purpose.

The instructions provided with the kit are relatively clear, although experience gained from other kit-building would be valuable, to assist with understanding the sequence of construction and the various folds and cutting required. I chose to add the brick lining supplied with the kit by cutting the lining

Fig. 74   The finished brick tunnel portal
with flat wing walls, constructed according
to the kit instructions.

Fig. 75 Superquick's tunnel lining sheet is shorter and more flimsy than the one in the Metcalfe kit; additional card bracing can be used to stiffen the lining before fixing to the layout.

paper in half along its longer axis to give two equal sections, one for each portal. The lining was glued into position after cutting all the individual tab liners and scoring all the joints. This was quite a tedious task, but, done neatly, resulted in a satisfying model.

As there is no card former for the tunnel section, the thin card used for the liner is prone to bending or folding. To reduce the risk of this, thick card strengthening pieces may be added at the bottom edge and on the rear face of the main tunnel portal section.

Once set, the printed brick arch and keystone parts are added to the face of the portal structure, overlying the tabs of the tunnel liner. This completes the kit, except for optional weathering and detailing with vegetation to blend the structure in to the layout.

If the kit is completed as per the instructions, then it can be used as a double track brick arch structure. With careful cutting, however, one portal could be combined with others to produce a multiple tunnel portal typical of an urban station approach. Brick retaining walls formed from card covered with brick paper from the same supplier could be used on either side of the portal, to extend the retaining walls or blend into cutting retaining walls.

Plaster Moulds

Plaster moulded tunnel portals are typically provided in a raw unpainted state for the modeller to finish and detail as required, which makes them quite adaptable. As an example, Woodland Scenics plaster mouldings were used to represent both concrete portals (cat. ref: C1152) and timber tunnel portals (cat. ref: C1154) for an N-gauge layout based on North American practice.

The detail of the Woodland Scenics plaster mouldings is very good, with crisp detail, particularly on the representation of the timber portals. Straight from the packet, the mouldings require very little work to clean up mould lines or waste material. The plaster mouldings need to be painted, and this is more easily done before fixing them to the layout. The choice of paint is down to the modeller, but acrylic paints tend to give the best results, as they soak into the plaster and dry quickly, but without obscuring the fine detail of the moulding.

To paint the timber portals, I started with a base mid-brown colour similar to that of a cedar wood. When this was dry, I built up from the base layer using lighter and darker shades to highlight the timber features of the portal. I then weathered the structure using various dark brown earth, black, charcoal and

Fig. 76 A Woodland Scenics plaster mould for a cast-concrete tunnel mouth, shown in N-gauge set in to the landscape of the layout.

Fig. 77 Another Woodland Scenics plaster mould product, also in N-gauge, this time representing a North American prototype timber structure.

grey shades, as well as green and yellow to represent aging of the timber, and black around the crown to represent smoke staining. The concrete portal mouldings were given a similar paint and weathering treatment, but using various shades of grey to represent pre-cast concrete blocks.

Once the painted mouldings had thoroughly dried they were ready to be fixed to the layout. This is best done by gluing small wooden blocks to the track bed first and then fixing the portal castings to the baseboard and the blocks. Before fixing it is important to check that the portal provides adequate clearance to the rolling stock, especially if using the portal at a slight angle to the track alignment.

It is important to note that the plaster mouldings can be very fragile and need to be handled with

Fig. 78 A timber portal tunnel painted with acrylics for the base colour and suitably blackened and weathered using dry-brushing techniques.

Fig. 79 An example of the concrete-style portal, weathered and with climbing vegetation added as part of the scenic setting.

care during preparation and painting, as well as when fixing the moulding to the baseboard. PVA or impact adhesive (for example, UHU) type glues are suitable for fixing and generally hold the mouldings firm to the baseboard. These types of adhesive can also be used to repair mouldings when any damage occurs. The plaster mouldings are soft enough to be cut or carved with a sharp craft knife, should the shape need to be altered to suit a particular location on the layout.

Ready-to-Plant Structures

A number of manufacturers provide ready-to-plant tunnel portal structures for model railway layouts, more commonly in OO-gauge. These include those produced under the Hornby Skaledale banner and

Fig. 80 Resin-cast ready-to-plant structures include this stone single-track portal in OO-gauge from the Hornby Skaledale range.

Scenecraft by Bachmann. Obviously, these structures save time during layout construction, and out of the box they can be seen to be good-quality detailed items, but they are a costlier option than kits or scratch-building.

Ready-to-plant structures can be used straight from the box and fixed to the layout using similar types of PVA or impact adhesives as for plaster moulds. The level of detail and quality of the painting on these structures is generally very good, although some might argue that the paint finish is slightly satin or gloss and could do with dulling down to make the structure appear more realistic. This is a personal choice for the modeller, but if required a wash with matt varnish or a weathering powder can tone down the finish. Additional painting and weathering can also make the structure more unique to a particular location and reduce the somewhat 'manufactured' look.

Often these types of structures are resin or stone cast, which will add significant weight to a layout. This may be an important consideration when building a portable layout for exhibition purposes.

Scratch-Building

The decision to build the tunnel portals and wing walls from scratch can be the result of a number of factors. If you are modelling a real location, the chances are that there will be no kit or ready-to-plant item that exactly matches the structure in the

Fig. 81 Before fixing the portal in place, paint and weather if necessary and source a couple of small timber off-cuts for additional support.

Fig. 82   Test-fit the portal to check track clearances at the location on the layout.

Fig. 83   Fix the portal in place, checking that it is vertical, and glue and screw small timber off-cuts to the baseboard to provide additional support.

Fig. 84   Test-fit the wing walls to the angle desired for the location on the layout.

Fig. 85 Fix the wing walls to the baseboard and portal with impact adhesive and if necessary use timber supports for these parts too.

prototype. Alternatively, the location on the layout may require a specific portal configuration, shape or style that is not available in kit form.

Scratch-building the tunnel portal and wing walls can be the best option to get a structure on the model layout that fully meets the modeller's requirements. With the availability of embossed plasticard in a wide variety of brick and stone representations, there is likely to be a style that will suit a particular need. A carcass for the structure can be formed from a cheaper readily available material such as plywood, card or foam board and this can be covered to provide a sturdy structure. An alternative would be to consider cast resin to form the bespoke tunnel portal, utilizing one of the resin moulding kits on the market.

POSITIONING PORTALS AND CHECKING CLEARANCES

Once the portal has been made or sourced and is ready to mount on the baseboard, it is useful to check its position relative to the planned landscape and track. Its proposed position can be drawn on to the board and various locations may be tested before making a final decision.

At this stage it is also important to check the clearances of the rolling stock planned for the layout. When this testing has been completed, the portal position should be accurately marked on the baseboard for fixing and then put to one side

for safety while the track bed is painted. Where appropriate or desired, the track is painted and if necessary a section into the tunnel mouth is ballasted to make it look more realistic. Depending on the scale being modelled, ballasting may or may not be necessary. Generally, for O–16.5mm and OO-gauge it is possible to effectively add ballast to the track after placing the portals in place, but before completing all of the scenery. However, for both OO9 narrow-gauge and N-gauge modelling, ballasting is more of challenge in a small space that is difficult to access. In these cases, it might be prudent to consider placing at least some of the ballast prior to fixing the tunnel in place.

When the painting and ballasting (where required) have been completed, the tunnel portal should be securely fixed to the baseboard. For plastic kits and plaster mouldings, this is best achieved by first gluing and screwing a small block of wood to the baseboard behind the line of the portal. Once set, the portal can be glued in place with an appropriate adhesive and left to set. The wooden blocks can then be used as support to the tunnel lining (see below).

TUNNEL LININGS

All tunnels have a lining, so adding a lining to a tunnel on a model layout will give a better representation of the real thing. Tunnel linings in real tunnels depend on the local geology and on the period when the

Fig. 86   The N-gauge plastic portals are supported in a similar way to the resin items; paint and weather the stonework before fixing, if required.

Fig. 87   Test-fit the portal to the baseboard and use timber off-cuts to support the portal wall in the permanent position.

Fig. 88   Fix the portal to the baseboard with impact adhesive, and the timber supports with white glue, and add the wing walls.

On my 4mm scale layout 'Llanfair & Meifod', a tunnel was used on the narrow-gauge line to allow the narrow gauge to turn back through a 180-degree turn and pass under the standard-gauge line underneath the scenery of the layout (see Fig. 32). The purpose of the tunnel was to create the illusion that the narrow-gauge line went somewhere off scene, when it actually returned via the loop to the same fiddle yard. This deception has certainly had the desired effect at exhibitions, where viewers have queried the route of the track and how it returns to the same fiddle yard unseen.

The tunnel and scenic effects on 'Llanfair & Meifod' were achieved using an open type of baseboard construction, with the standard (OO-gauge) track on a plywood track base, supported on softwood risers fixed into the main baseboard frame. The lower narrow gauge was laid on to a plywood solid base fitted to the bottom edge of the softwood frame for the baseboard. To achieve the clearances, measured at approximately 45mm height, to allow the narrow gauge to pass below the standard-gauge line, the standard gauge was laid to a gradient rising 20mm between points A and B (see Fig. 33) and then reduced by 20mm between B and C to get back to baseboard datum level for the layout.

This was a critical factor at the planning stage because the layout is designed as modular. It can be run with or without the dual-gauge sections and in various configurations, depending on the location where it is set up. The track position and level at points A and C are common to all four modules to ensure this modular system is maintained.

As well as the standard-gauge line being raised by 20mm, the narrow-gauge line was dropped by approximately 25mm within the baseboard framing, to create the clearances at the over-bridge (location B) and the tunnel section hidden below the scenery between B and C (see Fig. 33).

Fig. 89 *A scratch-built tunnel portal on the OO9 narrow-gauge section of 'Llanfair & Meifod' layout, made using embossed plasticard; the arch stones and key stone are formed from individual pieces of plasticard, cut out, painted and glued to the portal wall.*

Fig. 90 *Access to the narrow-gauge track tunnel on the right from the fiddle yard.*

Fig. 91   N-gauge stone tunnel with black card lining visible through the tunnel mouth; the track is ballasted into the tunnel mouth, to contribute to the realism of the model.

tunnel was built. In hard rock areas, where the tunnel may have been formed by blasting, the lining to the tunnel may just be the natural rock, possibly with a brick or concrete cover immediately inside the tunnel mouth. In softer rock or less competent materials, tunnels are fully lined using masonry or, in more recent times, concrete.

Lining a tunnel with brick or concrete is the most common method and this can be represented in a number of ways in model form. The simplest and quickest way is to assume that the inside of the tunnel is heavily weathered and distinguishing bricks

or concrete block is not possible. In this instance, the lining may be formed by a piece of card painted black.

The tunnels created on a model railway layout do not necessarily have to be fully lined, but ensuring that the lining extends far enough into the tunnel will maintain the illusion of the real thing. There are no rules as to the extent of lining needed and it will vary from location to location on a layout, governed by viewing angles and the scale of the model. On my N-gauge layout 'Duddeston Junction', for example, the tunnel lining was extended approximately 50mm from the back of the portal wall and the lining was

Fig. 92   Card lining formed from an old cereal packet, viewed from the inside of the spiral tunnel on an N-gauge layout.

formed from black card, curved to a profile to match the portal. To enhance the impression of a long dark gloomy tunnel, the baseboard around the track inside the tunnel was painted black, using cheap acrylic paints that dried quickly and covered the wood and polystyrene easily.

FORMING THE TRACK BED

The treatment of the track bed for the tunnel will depend on whether you have adopted a solid or open type of construction for the baseboard. On a solid baseboard, the track bed of the tunnel is limited only by the landscape to be modelled around it. The track alignment through the tunnel on a solid base-board should be marked and it can then be painted a dark colour to emphasize the gloom of the tunnel.

On an open-top baseboard structure the track bed can be formed from plywood. Ideally, it should be wide enough to allow for an area on either side of the track, to catch any rolling stock that might derail in the tunnel and prevent it falling through the layout.

CONSTRUCTING THE LANDSCAPE

Once the location of the tunnel on a layout has been decided, it is necessary to consider how the scenery through which the tunnel passes is to be formed. There are many ways to do this and many books have been written on the subject; one excellent example is Tony Hill's (2010). For the purposes of this book, however, I have provided a description of the methods that I have used on a number of layouts; these are not necessarily the 'best' methods, but they have worked for me and given the result I was looking to obtain.

Before constructing any landscape, it is important and beneficial to try to visualize what you are trying to create. Escape from the modelling room if possible and observe the landscape in the real world. Look at the shapes of the hills, trees, hedging and rocks, for example, taking note of their size relative to man-made objects such as buildings and walls. It is also useful to note that there are few perfectly straight lines in the natural world, so you will need to make the modelled scenery reflect the shape and curves realistically. It is also useful to observe the wide variety of colours in the real world – this does not necessarily include the luminous green that is sometimes seen on model railway layouts!

The visualization process can be assisted by photo-graphs of real landscapes, rural or urban, depending on the scene you are trying to create, as well as sketches of landscape features from a real location

Fig. 93 Observation of how the track bed is formed in the real world is very useful when trying to create the same in model form; note also the wide variety of colours in the scenery.

Fig. 94 Natural scenery has a wide range of shapes, colours and textures; when out and about, take photographs for reference when modelling layout scenery.

that you may wish to replicate in model form. A three-dimensional sketch or two of the landscape for the layout may also help. It is not essential to do this, but it can be useful to record your ideas, especially if you have to create the landscape over a long period. You do not need to be an artist and the sketches do not need to be perfect scale drawings; the idea is simply to have something to hand that enables you to visualize what you are trying to create.

Once you have your vision, you can start forming the basic shape of the scenery. Off-cuts of plywood and timber can be used as a basic skeleton; expanded polystyrene packaging is another very useful and lightweight alternative. With timber, the shape of the land can be formed using materials such as papier maché, chicken wire or plaster bandage, or a combination, with scrunched-up newspaper or waste paper between the timber formers to provide shape to the surface and to support the papier maché or plaster bandages until they are dry.

Expanded polystyrene can be carved using a hot wire cutter or an old carving knife to get a basic shape. This can then be overlaid with papier maché or plaster bandages to give the final shape of the ground. Whichever technique is used to form the landscape, the hard landscaping, such as tunnel portals, wing walls and retaining walls, should be fixed to the baseboard prior to adding the surface layers. The landscape modelling can then be moulded around these structures, making them appear to be a part of the scenery rather than randomly placed pieces of infrastructure. When adding rock outcrops in a rural setting, depending on size, this can be done either before the surface layers or pressed into the scenery while it is still wet and mouldable.

The scenery in an urban setting is sometimes easier to represent in model form, particularly because man-made structures are likely to feature more straight lines. In model form the urban setting can be created in the same way as a rural landscape, using simple timber formers or expanded polystyrene as a carcass on to which buildings and features such as retaining walls can be fixed.

I have used all of these techniques on layouts, but my preferred solution is the use of expanded

Fig. 95 The O-gauge layout 'Leamington Spa', by Pete Waterman: the careful selection of scenic materials, attention to detail and use of a variety of colours and textures all result in a realistic-looking model.

Fig. 96 The realistic rocky outcrop in the lane on my OO-gauge layout is created from polystyrene sheets, carved to form the shape of the scenery and then carefully painted and weathered with appropriate colours.

polystyrene overlaid with plaster bandages for rural landscapes. This gives a light but strong scenery shell as a base to a layout. For more urban settings, expanded polystyrene is good for the basic carcass, with embossed plasticard sheets being used for retaining walls and similar structures.

Once the scenery has been formed, the shell can be painted with suitable base colour paints such as grey, brown and green to represent rock, earth and grass respectively, depending on the location. This helps seal the base before adding scenic products and gives a base colour other than white. Of course,

Fig. 97 Plaster rock moulds, such as those from the Woodland Scenics range, offer good levels of realism. They can be used to represent outcrops on the side of a cutting, as in this example from an N-gauge layout.

Fig. 98 A realistic urban scene, with embankments and an over-bridge carrying a road and trams over the railway lines to the station approach; an OO-gauge layout by Tim Pollard.

if you plan to model chalk grassland areas, you can leave the basic shell white!

ACCESS FOR MAINTENANCE AND ROLLING STOCK RESCUE

All modellers should remember Tisdale's First Law of Model Railway Tunnels, which states: 'If a piece of rolling stock is going to derail and get stuck, it will be in a tunnel where you can't easily get at it!' Construction of tunnels on model railway layouts should where possible always consider the means of access, not only for the recovery of derailed rolling stock but also for track maintenance and cleaning. You do not want to be losing your precious rolling stock in an inaccessible tunnel, so you need to mitigate the risk.

Fig. 99   Access to the two-metre long tunnel on Tim Pollard's OO-gauge layout is from underneath the open-frame baseboard.

There are many varied and ingenious methods for creating access to a tunnel, including flaps or removable sections of scenery. One layout that featured hinged flaps was the N-gauge American-themed layout 'Pine Ridge Creek', where careful cutting of the plywood back scene allowed the use of the removed wood as the flap, with the addition of a couple of small brass hinges.

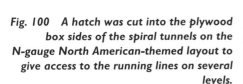

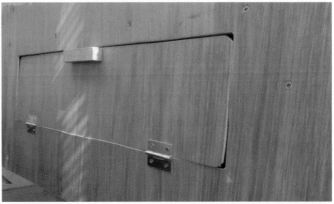

Fig. 100   A hatch was cut into the plywood box sides of the spiral tunnels on the N-gauge North American-themed layout to give access to the running lines on several levels.

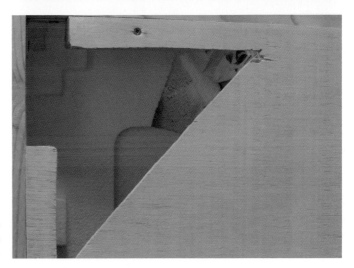

Fig. 101   To access the narrow-gauge tunnel on my OO-gauge layout, a hatch was cut in the underside of the baseboard.

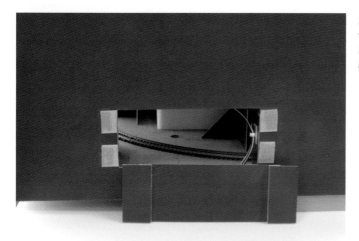

Fig. 102 An access hatch cut through the card side walls of the scenery on my N-gauge layout provides access to the lower-level loop.

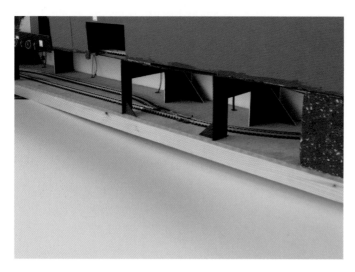

Fig. 103 At the rear of my N-gauge layout, the fiddle yard on the lower level is accessible along the entire length of the layout.

On 'Llanfair & Meifod', access to the narrow-gauge tunnel was achieved in a number of ways. Because of the open baseboard construction techniques used for the layout, it was possible to provide openings on the underside to access the track bed at a number of locations in the tunnel. This is one of the advantages of an open type baseboard construction. In addition, the design of the scenery above the tunnel at the fiddle-yard entrance allowed access to the first section of tunnel (see Fig. 90).

The design of my N-gauge layout 'Duddeston Junction' allowed access to the tunnels at either end of the layout through flaps in the framing, held in place by Velcro strips. On the operator side of the layout, the complete tunnel section is open to allow the operator to access the tracks and storage loops. For a more detailed description of the construction of the layout and formation of the tunnels, see later.

HIDDEN SIDINGS AND FIDDLE YARDS

For my N-gauge layout 'Duddeston Junction', tunnels were required for both levels of the layout as scenic breaks and also to disguise return loops and fiddle yards on each layer. The layout was initially built as a test track for my N-gauge locomotives and was laid as a single loop of track on a sheet of MDF (approximately 1.2m by 0.8m), utilizing track sections from a train set and a couple of pieces of flexi-track.

Inspired by a number of articles by other railway modellers in various magazines, including *Railway Modeller*, my test track quickly became the basis for a small N-gauge layout. My intention was to use this layout for testing rolling stock as well as for trying out ideas for scenic development for future layouts (*see* Chapter 7 for more detail on scenic ideas).

Starting with the lower level, which was the initial test track loop, the section of the loop that was formed largely from flexi-track became the viewing side of the planned layout. The mainly set-track section to the rear was to be hidden in a tunnel and would form the rest of the running loop and fiddle yard area at this level. Peco single-track stone tunnel portals (ref: NB-31) were used, painted suitable dull matt shades of grey and weathered appropriately, to

Fig. 104   One of the tunnel portals on the lower level of my N-gauge layout, providing access to the fiddle yard.

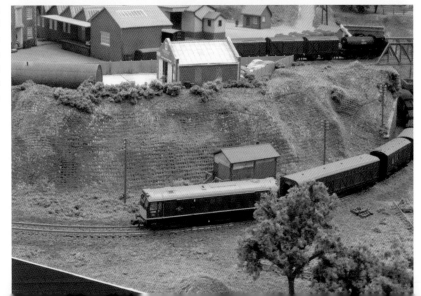

Fig. 105   The height between the lower and upper levels of my N-gauge layout was governed by the height of the tunnel portals and the thickness of the polystyrene tray from a train-set box.

disguise the return loop and create the impression of a line passing through the layout.

The upper level of the layout was set by the height of the tunnel portals and the thickness of the expanded polystyrene packaging from the train-set box, which was used as the main support material to the upper level. Before fixing the polystyrene to the baseboard, the area of the upper level was marked on to the board and used as a guide for the upper-level baseboard. The upper-level baseboard was formed from 2mm thick artist's mounting card, which can be cut easily using a heavy-duty craft knife and a steel straight edge.

After marking out the size of the upper level, the polystyrene packaging was then fixed to the MDF baseboard with PVA adhesive. The sturdy card for the upper level was mostly supported on the polystyrene and was fixed in place with PVA adhesive. At the rear of the layout, where the storage loop and the fiddle yard are located, the upper level was supported on 'trestles' made from the same thick artist's mounting card, with each trestle being cut to fit the location (see Fig. 103). Before fixing the upper-level baseboard in place the lower baseboard and supporting materials in the tunnels immediately behind the tunnel portals were all painted matt black,

to help disguise the tunnels and the non-prototypical curves of the return loops.

Once the tunnel portals for the lower level had been glued to the baseboard, the track on the lower level was ballasted through the viewing section and into the tunnel mouths for a distance of about 20 to 30mm. Once that element had been completed satisfactorily, the baseboard for the upper level was fixed in place. With the upper baseboard in position, back boards were then cut and shaped for all four sides of the main baseboard, to box in the lower level and provide back-scene boards to the upper level at each end of the layout. Access hatches were cut into the back-scene boards at each end before fixing to the layout to provide emergency access for cleaning and retrieving derailed stock. The cut-out sections of the card were then used to form hatches for each opening, held in place with Velcro strips, giving a lightweight but effective tunnel access.

The track on the upper level comprises a similar loop to that of the lower level, constructed from a combination of set-track sections and flexi-track. The loop differs in terms of size, fitting over the lower level in a smaller board footprint, but its construction is the same in principle. On the upper level, a section of the rear of the loop is screened off using

Fig. 106   The fiddle yard on the upper level sits behind the back-scene board and is accessed via tunnels at either end of the upper level.

Fig. 107 Hatches for the lower-level loop were cut through the card side walls with a heavy-duty craft knife and off-cuts of the same size were used to create overlaps on to which Velcro patches were glued.

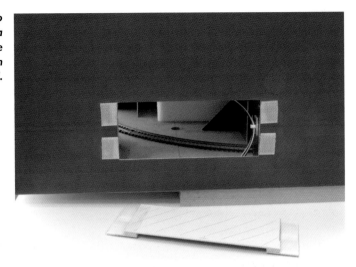

Fig. 108 With the hatch held firmly in place by the Velcro, the hatch fits flush and lets no light into the tunnels.

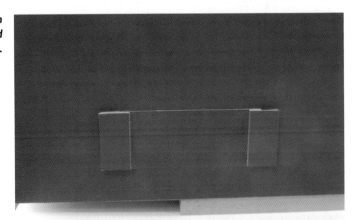

Fig. 109 At the entrance to the goods yard and factory sidings, a diamond crossing allows a head shunt to be included and enables shunting operations in the yard at the same time as trains using the upper circuit.

Fig. 110   A compact goods yard facility including goods shed and fuel depot, as well as two factory sidings, provide plenty of operational interest on this N-gauge layout.

a back scene, again formed using the same thick artist's card.

Although the upper level does not have a storage loop like the lower level, there is a hidden point that gives access to the industrial sidings and small goods yard that occupy the central part of the upper baseboard. The sidings are accessible via a hole in the back scene, with the track emerging from under a road over a girder bridge. The track at this point passes over a diamond crossing at the location of the girder bridge, which provides access to a hidden head shunt siding off scene, and allows the sidings to be operated independent of the upper-level loop. With this arrangement, it is possible to have up to three trains operating at any one time on the layout, with one on each of the lower and upper circuits and a third shunting the industrial sidings and yard. On such a small layout this ensures that there is always something moving in the viewable section.

On the left-hand side of the layout, when viewed from the front, the track on the upper level passes over a level crossing and immediately under a girder

bridge. A number of industrial buildings placed strategically at this point, and at a particular angle, prevents viewers at the front of the layout seeing where the train has disappeared under the road and industrial buildings.

Part of the upper-level loop was disguised by hiding it under the road and the industrial scene above the goods yard, which forms the backdrop to the entire layout. It is worth noting here that the multi-level approach used on this layout – stepping upwards to the back of the layout – adds depth and helps to create the impression of a layout that is much larger than it is in reality.

The careful use of acrylic paints, to provide a dull, overcast sky background, contributed to the urban theme of the layout. A collage effect of building outlines painted in various dull shades of brown and grey also helped to give depth to the urban landscape. The collage technique was extended to the use of pictures of real and drawn trees, added to the backscene with model trees planted on the layout in front.

Fig. 111 Access to the fiddle yard disguised by the oblique angle of bridge and track bed, as well as the road crossing.

Fig. 112 The strategic placement of factory buildings and chimney, as well as lots of fine detail, draw the viewer's eye away from the fiddle yard exit/ entrance on this side of the layout.

Returning to the construction of the tunnel to disguise the upper-level loop, on the right-hand side of the layout, the track passes under a stone road bridge, through a short but deep cutting with stone retaining walls before entering a tunnel portal under the residential area at this end of the layout.

Behind the back scene at the upper level is the head shunt for the industrial sidings and a section of the upper loop, all of which can be used as a fiddle yard to remove and place rolling stock on the tracks out of sight of the viewing public. Access to the tunnel on the upper level is via a number of appropriately sized

Fig. 113 A wider view of my N-gauge layout 'Duddeston Junction' shows the multi-level stepped urban scene, which suggests a much larger layout than the actual 1.2m by 0.8m baseboard dimensions.

Fig. 114 Clever use of full-relief buildings in the foreground, with low-relief structures behind and then a collage of buildings and tree cut-outs on the back scene, give a perspective of depth to the viewer.

Fig. 115 At the opposite end of the upper level to the view in Fig 112, the other exit/entrance to the fiddle yard is disguised by a road over-bridge, a short retaining wall cutting and then a portal below the residential area.

holes cut in the back-scene board. These allow the operator to reach any derailed stock and to clean the track. On the lower level the entire length of the track at the rear of the layout is open, to be used as a fiddle yard (see Fig. 102).

Retaining walls have been extensively used on this layout, to give the impression of a railway squeezed into an urban setting and competing for space with many other land uses. (The varied construction methods used for these retaining walls are described in more detail in Chapter 5.) The lower loop was intended to represent a secondary route through line, with a redundant and lifted junction at the front left-hand side of the layout providing the basis for the layout name. The upper-level loop was supposed to represent an industrial tramway system, built to a lower standard and only meant for operation by small, short-wheelbase shunting locomotives with a couple of wagons.

TRACK CLEANING

The track on this N-gauge layout is cleaned first with a traditional track rubber, then with Gaugemaster cleaning pads (ref: GM39), which clip to the axle of a wagon pulled or pushed around the layout by a loco. In my case, the wagon is a modified Peco 45T tank wagon kit, with most of the brake gear removed to accommodate the pad between the axles. It was painted in a different colour from the others to identify it as a track-cleaning vehicle!

This is an N-gauge example, but the same basic principles can be applied to other scales/gauges. In addition, ready-made track-cleaning vehicles are available in OO and HO. Examples of the HO variety are used extensively as a way of keeping the track clean on the magnificent layouts at Miniature Wonderland in Hamburg, Germany.

Fig. 116 Access for track cleaning on a small N-gauge layout can be a challenge; this track is kept clean using a wagon kit adapted to accommodate axle-hung cleaning pads.

Fig. 117 The cleaning wagon is painted to match the rolling stock and can be attached to the end of a train and pulled around the layout to polish the rail surfaces.

UNUSUAL TUNNELS

WORKING 'EMPTY' AND 'FULL' TRAINS

One modelling trick that is sometimes seen on exhibition layouts is the use of tunnels associated with industrial buildings or mines to give an impression of the loading and unloading of trains. The concept has been covered by a number of authors, including Michael Andress (1981), but an introduction to it follows here.

It is possible on the same layout to model two separate scenes that could be linked by a railway.

In the example shown here, the empty train arrives at the mine and disappears out of sight, reappearing at the other side of the layout as a train of empty wagons leaving an industrial processing plant. In the opposite direction, a train of empty wagons can be worked in to the industrial processing plant and then emerge via the tunnel at the mine end as a full train leaving the mine.

If the two trains of locomotive and wagons are identical, this reinforces the impression of an empty train arriving and filling up at the mine, transporting the mined product to a factory where full trains arrive and empty ones depart back to the mine.

Fig. 118   Attention to scenic detail, and use of proprietary kits and plasticard sheets that have been painted and subtly weathered with a range of natural shades, helps with creating realistic model infrastructure.

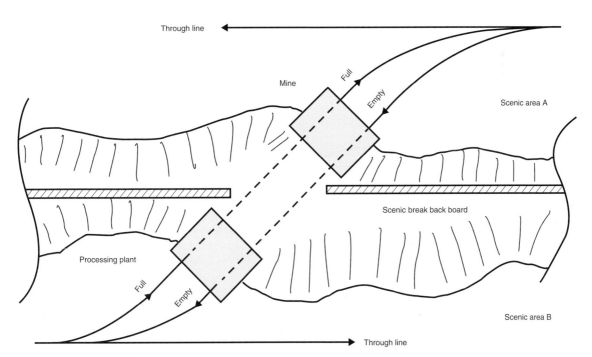

Fig. 119   Sketch concept for working 'full' and 'empty' trains through a mine and factory at opposite sides of a layout gives plenty of operational interest without physically handling the trains!

SPIRALS

The use of spirals on railways is not confined to the model layout. In real life, they have been used in a number of countries where the mountainous landscape makes railway construction a challenge. In model format, spiral tunnels can be used inside hills for trains to move between different levels of a layout and can save space in comparison with straight ramps. A number of suppliers sell spiral track bed kits or the feature can be made from scratch using a material such as plywood for the track bed.

Adding a spiral tunnel to a model railway can be a useful way of adding more running line length in a small space, especially where the layout baseboard size is constrained by the location. One example of the use of spiral tunnels is provided by the North American-themed layout 'Pine Ridge Creek', the work of the Jersey Model Railway Club (see Fig. 20). This N-gauge layout was constructed in 2012 to run a collection of North American, predominantly US,

locomotives and rolling stock that had been accumulated by the N-gauge team members.

A baseboard with integral legs had been built by one of the team for another project, but this had not come to fruition, so this ready-made baseboard was adopted for the American-themed layout. The baseboard was approximately 1.8m by 0.8m (about 6ft by 2ft 6in), so, to maximize the running length and to fit with a mountainous theme, the team looked at developing a figure-of-eight track plan, using a high-level bridge as the crossing point and a focal point in the centre of the layout for the viewing public. The bridge deck level was approximately 100mm above baseboard level. To get the track from the baseboard to this level at each end of the layout required the use of spirals at each end of the bridge.

A passing loop was provided at baseboard level, intended to represent a stopping point in the local town. Further additions included industrial sidings accessing grain silos and a mill complex at the front

Fig. 120 To increase the running length of this North American-themed N-gauge layout, a basic figure-of-eight track plan was enhanced by the use of a spiral track bed partially hidden in tunnels at either end of the layout.

Fig. 121   The N-gauge North American layout seen from baseboard level, showing the height needed to be attained in each spiral to reach the bridge abutments in the centre of the layout.

of the layout, to provide interest to the viewer. These features also helped to create a depth to the scenery, as almost the entire baseboard would be viewable, with no off-scene fiddle yard.

Once the track plan had been agreed and drawn up, the first stage of the layout construction was to build the spiral track-bed ramps to carry the line from baseboard level to the top of the bridge abutments. To keep the weight of the structure down, as well as the cost, the decision was taken to build the spiral track bed from plywood supported on off-cuts of softwood timber. However, before cutting the plywood for the track bed, it was necessary to establish a suitable gradient for the track. Various gradients were trialled using a plank of plywood with a piece of track temporarily fixed to it, gradually increased the gradient with blocks of wood under one end. For more advice on this process and the slightly more scientific method of calculating the

gradient, see Chapter 4, on constructing embankments.

For the American layout, it was determined that a gradient of about two degrees was acceptable and looked reasonable. This gave a running length of approximately 2.1m for the spirals at each end of the layout. To minimize joints in the track bed on the gradient and curves of the spiral section, each spiral section was to be formed, if possible, from a single piece of plywood. To achieve this aim, the track bed for each spiral was marked out on 4mm thick piece of plywood. A minimum track-bed width of 50mm was assumed and marked up accordingly. Each spiral section was then carefully cut by hand using a standard jigsaw, starting at the outer edge and following the inner line of the track bed as marked on the sheet of plywood. It should be noted that the size of the plywood sheet used for each spiral was about the same size as the narrowest edge of the baseboard,

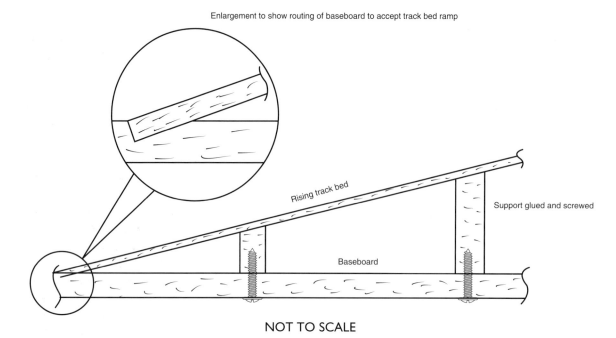

Enlargement to show routing of baseboard to accept track bed ramp

Rising track bed

Support glued and screwed

Baseboard

NOT TO SCALE

Fig. 122   Sketch cross-section showing the rising spiral gradient and the routing of the baseboard to accommodate the spiral track bed.

namely 0.8m, so that the start of the spiral was just within the dimensions of the baseboard surface.

When the spiral track bed had been cut out, it proved to be quite flexible, so it needed to be carefully adjusted to prevent it snapping. Each of the spirals was gently pulled open slowly to the height of the

bridge abutments. Off-cuts of softwood timber were used as supports for the track bed and to improve the strength of the structure. The supports were positioned at every 10–15mm increase in height, starting close to the bottom of the ramp and gradually working up to the level of the bridge abutments.

Fig. 123   With the spiral track beds fixed in place, landscape scenery was formed from polystyrene blocks and expanded foam sheets, prior to covering with plaster-impregnated bandages for the surface layer. A hatch gives access to the spiral at two different levels.

The timber formers were glued and screwed to the main baseboard surface and then the track bed was glued and screwed to each former, starting at the bottom of the spiral and working up.

To make sure that there was no step between the main baseboard surface and the surface of the spiral ramp track bed, a small section of the main baseboard, approximately 20–25mm along the direction of the spiral ramp from the starting point of the ramp, was routed out to a depth of about 4mm. The depth of the routing should be approximately equal to the thickness of the plywood track bed. The lower end of the spiral ramp was subsequently glued and screwed directly to the main baseboard in this slot. When fixed in place, the end of the plywood spiral was planed and sanded to achieve a smooth transition surface from the baseboard to the spiral ramp.

The top edges of each of the softwood timber formers were cut at a slight angle to reflect the gradient of the ramp and ensure that they supported the track bed without creating flat 'steps' in the ramp when the plywood was screwed to each former block. With the last support block in place, the spiral should end up at the same or close to the level of the bridge abutments. A short section of plywood was then cut to fit to bridge the gap between the top of the spiral and the wooden former supporting the back of the bridge abutments.

With both of the spiral sections in place, the track was glued and pinned to the plywood and baseboard, following the agreed track plan. The track was then wired and tested before any of the scenery elements of the layout were added. With this task completed, the next stage was to plan where the tunnel sections and open ledge sections of the track bed would be located. Placement of the tunnel sections was done at random to create short sections of ledges for the track through the mountainous scenery that had been planned.

With the track laid and tested, the next step was to place the tunnel portals for the layout at the correct locations. The portals used for the tunnel entrances on this layout were all plaster-cast moulds from the Woodland Scenics range, available in packs of two. The plaster castings are supplied unpainted, and are quite delicate and fragile, so they need to be handled with care. The portals for 'Pine Ridge Creek' were painted before use with acrylic paints, starting with a base colour, followed by dry brushing with a range of other colours to weather the structures as appropriate. Two different types of tunnel portal were utilized on 'Pine Ridge Creek', one group representing timber structures (Woodland Scenics ref: C1154) and the other group moulded to represent cast-concrete structures (Woodland Scenics ref: C1152).

Fig. 124 The centrepiece at the front of the layout is the mill complex, with silos all scratch-built from card and spray painted white.

Fig. 125 *The trestle bridge in the centre of the figure-of-eight track plan, connecting the upper end of each spiral, is set at least 100mm above the baseboard level.*

The position of each portal was marked on the track bed using a pencil and then small wooden blocks to provide supports to the portals were formed from off-cuts of planed softwood timber. Each support block was trimmed to size for the location, ensuring that it would not encroach upon the rolling stock. The blocks were then glued and screwed to the track bed. Once the blocks were set in position, the painted tunnel portal castings were carefully glued to both the track bed and the timber support blocks using PVA-type adhesive. Each portal was held in position with various tools and pieces of wood until the glue had set hard.

With the tunnel portals glued in place, the next step was to ballast the track on the open rocky ledges and into the tunnel mouths. Where appropriate, the wooden support blocks and the surrounding track bed were painted dark brown or black to make the tunnel interior appear dark.

Although this book does not cover bridge construction in any detail, the creation of the high-level bridge on 'Pine Ridge Creek' is relevant to the construction of the spirals and tunnels. The bridge forms the centrepiece of the layout and is certainly in a prime location, set at least 100mm above baseboard level. The bridge was formed from modified Ratio N-gauge trestle bridge kits (Ratio ref: 240 and 241), with the steel 'girders' used under the bridge deck

and not above as supporting trestles for the deck. The deck was painted to represent heavily weathered timber.

On this layout, as with all of the N-gauge layouts at the Jersey Model Railway Club, the track joints all have a tiny drop of solder applied to the outside of the rail, across the rail joint, to improve electrical conductivity on the running tracks. However, as a result of this practice, and as is the case with welded track in the real world, it was necessary to create a gap in the track on the circuit to accommodate rail expansion as a result of changes in temperature at the clubhouse. The easiest way to do this was to make the bridge removable. When the layout is in use, the bridge sits securely on the abutments and the central supporting trestle and is held in place with rail joiners at each end to the track on the spirals, which also provides electrical continuity to the track on the bridge. When the layout is not in use, the bridge is lifted off the layout and safely stored in a box to protect it. The resultant gap at the top of each spiral is sufficient to allow the rails to expand and contract without causing any damage.

With the track infrastructure in place, the layout was tested to ensure it was all working correctly prior to starting any of the scenery development. The points were motorized, with motors mounted on the baseboard top because of the integral folding

Fig. 126 Red LED buffer stop lights and scratch-built LED two-aspect light signals on the passing loop, which work with the points changing, add interest for the viewer.

legs of the baseboard. The motors were hidden beneath strategically placed lineside huts and the wiring was laid with the intention of burying it in the scenery once it had been added. Two-aspect colour light signals were scratch-built by one of the team for the passing loop at main board level, while red warning lights were added to the buffer stops at the mill complex right at the front of the layout, using commercially available kits from Gaugemaster (ref: GM58).

Before adding the scenery, back boards were cut and screwed to all sides of the layout baseboard. The boards were formed from 4mm plywood that had been cut to give a suitable shape to match the intended profiles of the finished scenery. This was not planned as such, but the location of the high points was governed by the presence of the tunnels. At this stage it was also necessary to consider future access to the tracks for cleaning, maintenance and the rescue of derailed rolling stock. Access to the spiral track beds at each end of the layout was essential and a further consideration in the design of the scenery.

On the left-hand side of the layout, as seen from the main public viewing side, one large hatch was cut in the plywood back board at the rear of the layout, giving access to the main tunnel sections on two levels of the spiral. After carefully marking the hatch, then drilling each corner, a small bladed jigsaw was used to cut out the hole in the plywood in one place and thus provide the wood for the hatch on completion.

A similar hatch was formed in the scenery back board at the end of the layout, on the short side of the baseboard. In this instance, the piece of plywood that had been removed was not used as the hatch, but instead provided a template for cutting a piece of clear perspex to match the hole. The idea was to add more interest for the viewing public by allowing them to observe trains passing through the tunnel. This is particularly effective for locomotives that have directional headlights.

Improving the internal view of the track bed in the tunnel meant modelling the tunnel wall and roof using card. Rock outcrops formed from plaster casts from the Woodland Scenics range were then fixed to this with PVA-type adhesive. The remaining tunnel sections on this side of the layout are shorter and easy to access from the portals.

The scenery was then formed within the boxing created by the back boards, using expanded polystyrene packaging materials recycled from various sources, including those typically found in model railway train set boxes. It is a good use of these materials, which have already been paid for and may otherwise simply be thrown away. Card formers were also used with the polystyrene to provide the basic shape of the scenery and in some areas

Fig. 127   The plywood side of the layout was carefully marked and cut using a jigsaw to form a hatch access to the spiral at one end of the layout; the removed piece of plywood was then mounted on hinges, to fold back in to the hole.

Fig. 128   At the opposite end of the same layout, the hole was cut in the plywood in the same fashion, but the removed piece was then used as a template to create a clear perspex hatch.

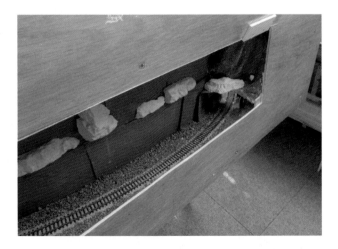

Fig. 129   The tunnel walls and roof were formed using card and plaster rock moulds to represent an uneven, unlined rock tunnel.

scrunched-up paper was also used as support for the overlying plaster bandage. Once the basic form of the scenery was achieved, plaster-impregnated bandage strips were used to cover the surface and then allowed to dry and harden off, to give a strong outer shell for the scenery.

To provide additional lining behind the tunnel portals, simple liners were formed, Blue Peter style, using card from recycled cereal packets. On the right-hand side of the layout, most of the tunnel sections were relatively short. Here, card linings were cut to the full length of the tunnels, to ensure that any derailed/errant stock was kept on the tracks and guided to the portals rather than into the depths of the scenery.

When all of the scenery had been formed, the surface was painted with matt emulsion, using green, brown and grey shades for grass, earth and rock areas respectively. When the paint had dried, surface texture was added using a variety of scatter materials from the usual suppliers. Hundreds of trees were then planted on the layout using bulk packs from the Bachmann Scene Scapes range. Wild horses, deer and a couple of bears were also added among the vegetation, providing some extra entertainment for youngsters and their parents, as they compete to see who can find the bears first!

UNDERGROUND RAILWAYS

Underground railways take the tunnel concept to the extreme, with not only track but also stations, sidings and other infrastructure all located in tunnels. Models of underground railway systems are a bit unusual. 'Gants Hill', modelled by my colleague Derek Lawrence and his friends, is one such layout, based loosely on the London Underground station of the same name in East London.

'Gants Hill' is OO-gauge and DCC-controlled and includes Central Line tube stock, District Line

Fig. 130 A plaster-cast concrete tunnel portal used on one of the many tunnels on the spiral of the N-gauge layout.

surface stock and trams in the High Street above the station. The tube and surface line rolling stock comprises stock entirely constructed from resin kits (my contribution to the layout), while the trams are converted static models.

The Central Line tube lines extend from a surface station via ramp sections in tunnels at either end of the layouts to Gants Hill underground station. The underground section is viewed via a window in the front of the layout, showing the station in detail, connecting to the station concourse at street level via an escalator. The tunnel for the station is formed from a section of plastic pipe of the correct diameter for the viewed side of the station to give the arched roof and platform layout.

One of the main challenges on this layout related to achieving a suitable angle for the access ramps at each end of the layout, to allow the tube-line rolling stock to negotiate it as full eight-car sets. The first two attempts worked with four-car sets but unfortunately proved to be too steep for an eight-car set. The ramps at each end of the layout are currently being redesigned and the entire underground station raised by about 30–40mm, to reduce the gradient of the running lines.

Fig. 131 A high-level view of the surface railway station on the London Underground railway-themed OO-gauge layout 'Gants Hill', by Derek Lawrence, set in East London in the 1950s.

Fig. 132 'Gants Hill' again: central and side power rails modelled using Code 60 rail added to standard Code 100 track for the surface section of the District Line approach to the station.

Fig. 133 Central Line tube lines exit Gants Hill station and descend to the underground section of the layout.

Fig. 134 Tunnel portals for the Central Line tube lines at the entrance to the ramp to the underground section on 'Gants Hill'.

Fig. 135   Cut-away section through the underground station on the lower level of the 'Gants Hill' layout, formed inside a plastic pipe.

Fig. 136   Close-up of the concourse area in the underground station on 'Gants Hill', with the escalators to the surface on the right; all lit by LEDs.

Fig. 137   Underneath the street-level baseboard of 'Gants Hill', showing the exit from the underground station to the ramp; in operation, the Central Line trains can be run in both directions on a continuous loop.

Fig. 138   Metal and timber framing was used for the ramp sections at each end of the 'Gants Hill' layout.

CHAPTER FOUR

BUILDING EMBANKMENTS

USE OF EMBANKMENTS

Railway embankments are used in the real world for a number of purposes and can be employed on model railway layouts in the same way. They are particularly useful in maintaining the gradient of a track bed over low-lying areas along the alignment of the railway, as an alternative to constructing a bridge or viaduct. In model form, this type of structure is particularly relevant on a scenic, rural-themed layout.

The construction of an embankment as part of a layout allows the modeller to create a significant landscape feature and assist in creating the impression of an accurate representation of a railway in the scenery, making it appear more realistic than a train set. An added advantage of this type of structure is that it also provides the modeller with the opportunity to show off locomotives and rolling stock.

Embankments have also been used by railway engineers where there was a need to construct crossings and junctions between different running lines at different levels. The embankment in this scenario enables a railway line to either rise or descend between different levels. The same principle can be applied to tracks on a model railway layout. The concept of using embankments in this way is particularly useful when building a layout in a confined space, as it can allow for the creation of a second level to a layout and potentially accommodate more running line in the same footprint.

An embankment that can be used to carry a line up to or down to another level is particularly relevant to an urban location. This type of feature has been used in the real world for the same purpose as on a model layout, namely to separate running lines vertically and to connect between different levels on a network. When using an embankment as a way of

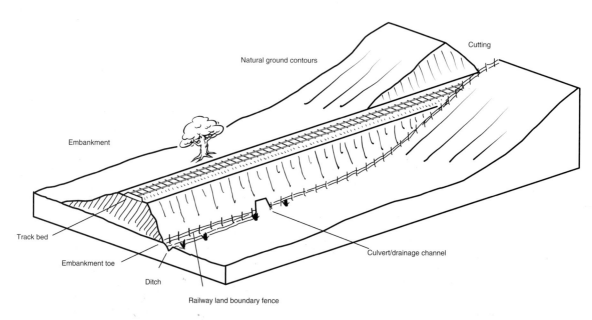

Fig. 139   A sketch three-dimensional diagram to show a typical embankment structure, based on a sketch in Fig. 7.8 of the N-Gauge Society Handbook.

connecting different levels, it is critical to ensure that the gradient of the embankment on the connecting line is correct, so that the locomotive will be able to negotiate the embankment with a train in tow.

BASEBOARD CONSIDERATIONS

Before looking at constructing an embankment, it is helpful to consider the type of baseboard that will be used, as this can influence layout plans and the choice of embankments and other railway infrastructure. Generally, baseboards are either solid or of the open-frame type (see Chapter 2).

A solid baseboard represents the traditional method of construction and begins with the building of a frame, typically from softwood or plywood. With the frame built, a surface board is created, often made from good-quality plywood of 6mm or 9mm thickness.

An open-frame baseboard is constructed in more or less the same way as the solid one. With the layout plan finalized and the location of the track bed and key landscape features of your layout decided, a softwood timber or plywood frame for the baseboard area can be built.

Once the frame has been built, the track bed can be cut from the chosen base material and fixed to the frame, using supporting pieces of timber as risers

Fig. 140   Observation of the shape and structure of a railway embankment, such as this one at Buckfastleigh on the South Devon Railway, will aid in creating similar structures on a model layout.

Fig. 141   Note the shallow embankment slope angles, and the variety and colours of the vegetation, as well as lineside detail, all of which can be copied in model form to make the model infrastructure more realistic.

Fig. 142   *On this extensive OO-gauge layout 'Newcastle', by Tim Pollard, an embankment is used across one end of the layout to carry a connecting line between the main level and an upper-level suburban branch line.*

Fig. 143   *The intermediate suburban station on 'Newcastle', by Tim Pollard, is on a low embankment above the scenic fiddle yard.*

Fig. 144   *The branch line on Tim Pollard's 'Newcastle' continues along the embankment, crossing the main line on an impressive multi-span girder bridge to the branch terminus station.*

where necessary. This will allow track beds to rise and/or fall within the framework, for the creation of embankments and cuttings. It is also useful at this stage to add additional formers fixed to the frame, to help with the creation of the layout scenery.

CONSTRUCTION

DETERMINING THE GRADIENT

In the real world, the construction of an embankment for a railway line was a major engineering task, requiring considerable planning and engineering assessment of the ground conditions prior to works commencing. An embankment would allow the gradient of the track bed to be kept to a reasonable level, with locomotives being able to travel along the lines relying on adhesion to the rails as a result of weight. This would obviate the need for additional measures such as rack-and-pinion cog arrangements, such as that used on Snowdon Mountain Railway in North Wales.

For model railway layouts, the same principles need to be applied. The model locomotive moves

Fig. 145   *An example of an old railway embankment on the approach to the former Princetown Station on Dartmoor; the embankment still retains its original slopes and an example of a cattle creep culvert, all good detail to note for a model.*

Fig. 146 A more extreme example of an embankment on the mid-section of the Snowdon Mountain Railway on the approach to a bridge over the footpath to the summit; note the steeper slope angles and sparse vegetation cover.

along the track and can climb gradients to a degree, but its capacity to climb is limited by the electric motor, the weight of the locomotive and its ability to adhere to the rails. Often, modellers will add ballast to a locomotive to increase its weight and thus improve track adhesion. However, the limitations of the model locomotive need to be recognized and there is a gradient of track beyond which the loco- motive will not be able to operate when pulling a train.

The gradient that model locomotives can easily negotiate will vary from model to model. When planning to use gradients on a layout, it is a good idea to test the locomotives that you intend to use on it before designing the embankment gradient. Once

you have determined the maximum gradient that is likely to be suitable, you can think about laying track on the layout.

A simple way to check the suitable gradient is to fix a length of track to a board and then use blocks of wood to raise one end of the board to create a gradi- ent. The locomotives can be tested on this length of track to see how they perform in terms of traction. Remember it is necessary to check the locomotives with a representation of the sort of train load that you are expecting them to pull up the gradient, not just running as a light engine.

In order to construct an embankment as an alternative to a bridge or viaduct on a layout on an open-frame baseboard, the track bed can be raised

Fig. 147 A simple test bed for working out suitable gradients for rolling stock; blocks of different sizes and in different positions can be used to increase or decrease the gradient.

and the corresponding ground contours lowered. This will create a low-lying area in the scenery within the open frame.

STARTING CONSTRUCTION

It is important when constructing an embankment to make sure that you have a solid base for the track bed to ensure that the locomotives and rolling stock will be able to travel along the track safely and easily. To form an embankment, start with the track bed using a piece of thin plywood, say 4mm thick, supported on risers made from timber off-cuts. The risers can be either fixed to the cross-bracing of an open baseboard or glued and screwed to a solid baseboard top.

With the track bed secured in place and tested, to ensure smooth running of the rolling stock, the next step is to form the embankment side slopes. If the layout is intended to be transportable, the aim should be to keep the fill material strong and lightweight. If the layout is to remain in a fixed location, the weight of the material used is less of an issue, the only limiting factor being the strength of the baseboard support structure.

MATERIALS

In the real world, railway engineers have used a wide variety of materials to construct railway embankments, including clay, gravel and broken rock. The selected materials were laid and compacted in layers

Fig. 148 Construction of an approach embankment to a viaduct on a large N-gauge layout, with plywood track bed fixed to softwood timber supports. JERSEY MODEL RAILWAY CLUB

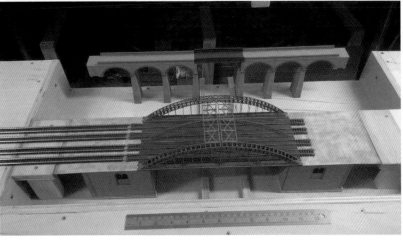

Fig. 149 A lowered section of baseboard built to accommodate a valley section, with the four-track main line on an embankment and bowstring girder bridge in the foreground, and the branch line on a stone and girder viaduct to the rear.

JERSEY MODEL RAILWAY CLUB

Fig. 150   Photographs of real railway embankments will help with model creation; note the variety of vegetation cover and low stone abutments for the girder bridge.

to form a stable base for the track bed. In model form, similarly, there is a variety of ways in which to create an embankment, and a number of different materials that may be used.

The sides of an embankment on a layout can be formed in a number of ways, always bearing in mind what the feature would look like in reality. Reference to photographs and books is really helpful to understand this and to create realistic-looking slopes. The embankment itself can be formed using timber risers fixed to the open framing or baseboard, or lightweight materials such as polystyrene blocks to create the height. A track bed formed from thin plywood can be fixed to the top of the timber risers, or, where polystyrene is used, the track can be laid directly on to this material. Alternatively, a thin strip of cork may be placed under the track alignment if preferred.

In my experience, the best results can be obtained by using plaster-impregnated bandage as the main surface covering. The best (and usually the cheapest) product for this is marketed for use by artists producing sculpture, and may be sourced from an art

Fig. 151   Example of a low embankment built along the valley side, with land rising to the right and falling to the left of the picture; note the vegetation colours and variety.

Fig. 152   *Plaster-impregnated bandage is a good material to use when forming an embankment and other landscape on a model railway.*

materials shop. A number of suppliers, such as Peco (ref: PS-36), Woodland Scenics (ref: WC 1191, 1192) and Gaugemaster (Mod Roc ref: GM100), produce similar products, but they tend to be more costly.

Plaster-impregnated bandages offer a quick and effective way of forming the side slopes of embankments, as well as having wider scenic applications for creating ground contours. I have used this type of material many times on different layouts, for example, where I have used timber risers and plywood to form the track bed and where I have

used polystyrene to form the landscape on a layout. Where timber risers and plywood are used, the plaster bandage can be applied in strips, working along the embankment from one end with the strips overlapping each other to ensure no gaps.

It is often necessary to used scrunched-up paper below the bandage to support it to the shape that you want until it has dried and formed a hard shell. After this, the paper can be removed if required. It is also possible to use card formers, cut to the rough profile of the embankment and fixed parallel

Fig. 153   **The track-bed supports, made from softwood off-cuts, are set out on the baseboard surface and their locations are marked with a pencil.**

Fig. 154   **The track-bed supports should ideally be equally spaced along the alignment of the embankment to provide adequate support to the track bed.**

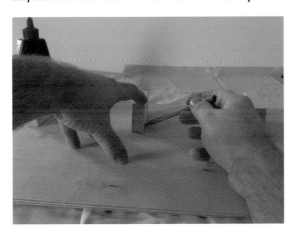

Fig. 155   Use a good-quality wood glue to fix the supports to the baseboard and ideally a couple of wood screws as well.

Fig. 156   When the supports are fixed to the baseboard, apply wood glue to the upper surface of the supports.

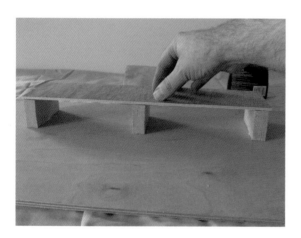

Fig. 157   Position the track bed and check the alignment; if required, use wood screws to hold the track bed firm on the supports.

Fig. 158   Prepare formers for the embankment slopes using stiff card.

Fig. 159   Insert and glue the formers to the baseboard and track-bed supports.

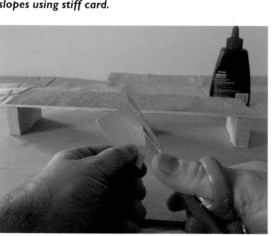

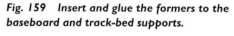

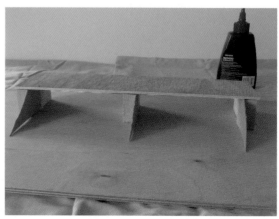

Fig. 160   Add scrunched-up packing paper to get an approximate idea of the desired shape of the embankment.

Fig. 161   All the paper packing in position between the formers and wedged under the track bed; if necessary, use a spot of white glue to hold the paper in place until the surface layers have been added.

Fig. 162   Open the plaster bandage rolls and, estimating the length of strip required, cut a number of strips ready to use; keep them in a plastic tub if this helps control the mess!

Fig. 163   Have about 20mm of tap water in an old plastic food container, then dunk a strip at a time into the water for a few seconds before use.

Fig. 164   Starting at one end, apply the first strip and tease it with your fingers to get the shape you want; it will set hard as it dries.

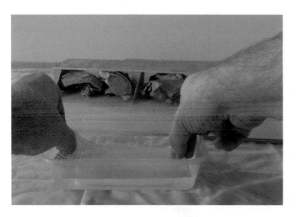

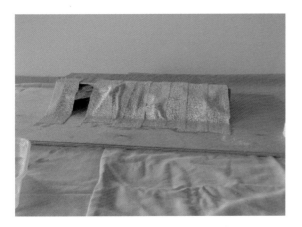

Fig. 165 Work your way along the embankment, making sure each new strip overlaps for a few millimetres with the next strip.

Fig. 166 Once all the strips for the section have been added, and while they are still wet, the slopes can be carefully teased to the desired shape. Extra layers of plaster bandage can be added as required and then it can be left to dry.

to the track bed, as additional support to the plaster-bandage surface layer.

Where expanded polystyrene is used to form embankments and other elements of the ground contours of the scenery, it needs to be carved to the approximate shape of the scenery prior to placing the plaster bandage surface covering.

One alternative method of creating an embankment is to use timber formers and plywood for the track bed, then chicken wire to create the basic slope shapes. The wire is fixed to the wooden frame and the track bed using a staple gun and can then be covered in papier maché or plaster-impregnated bandage (for example, Modroc) to produce a hard shell, as before.

This method tends to be less flexible than the others in shaping the ground contours. In addition, shaping and cutting the wire for fixing to the timber requires extreme care. Cut the wire with hard wire cutters and be very aware of the sharp edges that

Fig. 167 Lowering a section of the solid baseboard to form a valley on this N-gauge layout required the creation of an embankment approach to each side of the bowstring girder bridge.

JERSEY MODEL RAILWAY CLUB

you will get. The use of protective gloves and goggles or safety glasses is definitely recommended.

When forming an embankment on a solid baseboard, the track bed will need to be raised, or a section of the baseboard will have to be dropped below the main board level, supported on a timber frame. The embankment may then be built across the lowered board. This technique was adopted for the main-line N-gauge layout at Jersey Model Railway Club (see also Fig. 149). It allowed for the inclusion of a feature bow-string bridge structure and approach embankments for the four-track main-line circuit, as well as a single-track branch line, which was partially on an embankment and partially on a stone viaduct across the front of the layout.

READY-TO-PLANT STRUCTURES

All the above methods assume that the modeller will be building embankments on their layouts from a selection of raw materials. However, it is also possible to buy ready-formed polystyrene block sections of embankment, including the range of products available from Woodland Scenics (for example, the risers, ref: WST 1406). The range and how to use them are all explained in a handy guide (Woodland Scenics ref: WST 1402).

The advantage of products such as those offered by Woodland Scenics is that they simply need to be placed on the layout and the track bed (also available from the same supplier) laid on top. The addition of side slopes or retaining walls to the embankment will still be required, as well as painting and the use of scatter materials to create any vegetation.

In the smaller gauges, such as N and Z, some manufacturers even supply ready-to-plant structures with the track bed coloured appropriately and 'vegetation' in the form of grass to the embankment sides. This leaves little for the modeller to add, except the track and rolling stock.

EXAMPLES OF EMBANKMENT PROJECTS

AN EMBANKMENT ON AN OO9 LAYOUT

For the OO9 micro-layout 'Gylchfan', I created a circular track layout based loosely on a Welsh narrow-gauge theme set somewhere in the Welsh Marches area of the UK. Starting at the front left-hand side of the layout, the track exited the fiddle

Fig. 168 The embankment on the right above the retaining wall on my OO9 micro-layout 'Gylchfan' was created using the techniques shown above, with polystyrene and scrunched-up paper packing.

Fig. 169 Further extension of the hillside up from the railway embankment on 'Gylchfan' was achieved using the same landscape techniques. A culvert was incorporated in the embankment for scenic interest.

yard under an over-bridge built from leftover pieces of Wills dressed-stone sheeting (Wills ref: SSMP202). On the inside of the track, the ground level rose sharply with a brick retaining wall at the bridge abutment, giving way to hillside as the line traversed to the front of the layout. The land fell away from track level outside the track alignment and, after passing over a culvert, continued on a low embankment partially retained by stone walls as far as the railway crossing.

The layout was constructed using a solid 9mm plywood base approximately 550mm square, on to which I glued a 25mm thick sheet of expanded polystyrene using PVA-type adhesive. This would form the track-bed level for the layout. Thin balsa wood strip was then used to form a 'box' around all four

sides of the baseboard, to protect the polystyrene. I then marked a circle on to the polystyrene with an approximate diameter of 450mm, corresponding to the alignment for the inside rail of the track and the minimum radius that I wanted for the rolling stock that would be used on the layout.

To achieve the ground contours for the embankment and culvert, the polystyrene sheet was carved away with a sharp knife to give a rough idea of the final shape. The sections of Wills stone sheet used to represent the retaining walls were painted and then fixed in place.

For the adhesive, I opted to use a PVA glue so as not to melt the polystyrene sheet. To form the bridge deck for the culvert, I used a piece of the thin balsa wood sheet, as used around the sides of the

Fig. 170   Overall view of the OO9 micro-layout 'Gylchfan', showing the scenic detail. When the plaster shell was dry, the surface was painted various brown and grey base colours before the scenic ground cover was added.

layout, to fit between the polystyrene walls each side of the area cut out for the culvert. The culvert was adapted from the Wills kit (ref: SS38) and built in position after it had been painted.

Once the bridge and retaining wall sections were secured in place, the polystyrene was given a base coat using a selection of grey, brown and green emulsion paints to seal the surface before applying the plaster bandage to form the slopes. When the bandage strips had set dry, this was then painted with the same range of emulsion paints.

Scenic scatter materials from the Woodland Scenics range were added to build up the finished ground cover. Finishing touches included the painting and placement of individual pieces of shredded cork to represent rocks on the bank and valley sides, as well as the stream bed, while long grasses and tufts indicated poorly drained areas around the culvert.

EMBANKMENT ON AN OO-GAUGE LAYOUT

For the construction of an embankment on my OO-gauge 'Llanfair & Meifod' layout, I used an open-frame baseboard for the section of the layout that included the standard- and narrow-gauge

Fig. 171   Underside of the open-frame baseboard on my OO-gauge 'Llanfair & Meifod' layout, showing the polystyrene sheets and scrunched-up paper used between the plywood track beds.

Fig. 172 On the viewing side, the embankment for the standard-gauge track passes over the narrow-gauge track on a girder bridge, similar to the real life example.

interchange and the dual-gauge track sections. The reason for using an open-frame baseboard was to keep the weight down – it would be a relatively large baseboard section – and to allow for the creation of the various levels of track bed on the layout for both the standard- and narrow-gauge systems.

In line with the general concepts for construction, the track bed on this section of the layout was formed from 4mm plywood, supported on timber formers of varying sizes derived from off-cuts of the timber used for the main baseboard construction. This provided a basic skeleton structure around which the embankment could be formed.

For this particular example, I used scrunched-up pieces of paper, supplemented where necessary with card formers, to provide the basic shape of the ground contours. Plaster-impregnated bandage strips soaked in water were then used over the paper and card formers to form the ground contours, with the scrunched-up paper providing support to the bandages while they were still wet. At this stage, the material may be manipulated to get the desired ground contour shapes – have a bowl of water handy to wash your hands after this process!

Once they have dried, the plaster bandages set hard and provide a lightweight but strong shell as the basis for the landscape scenery. When it has dried and hardened off, the material is white, so, before applying any scenic detail, it is advisable to paint the landscape with a matt emulsion of an appropriate base colour, such as grey, brown or green. I tend to use various shades of all three colours to represent different rock types (grey), soils or earth (brown) and grass or vegetation (green).

CHOOSING APPROPRIATE COLOURS

It is important to choose appropriate colours, both for the base coat painting and, ultimately, for the overlying scenic treatment, so that the overall effect looks natural. I have seen many good model railway layouts spoilt by the use of very bright, artificial-looking colours – especially green – that bear no relation to the subtle shades observed in the real world.

To help you achieve a realistic-looking layout, with a palette of colours that matches those in the natural world, it is a good idea to get outside and observe the wide range and subtle differences in shades and colours in the fields, woods and hills. If possible, take photographs to record what you see, and refer to them when applying paint to your model railway landscape.

There is a wide range of colours and shades of materials available from many different suppliers. If they do not have the specific shade you want, you can mix and blend different colours to get closer to the effect you are trying to recreate. Remember, you do not have to be a professional artist to create a believable landscape scene on your layout, and experimenting with blends is a useful practice.

Fig. 173 The rising track embankment for the branch line on Tim Pollard's OO-gauge layout, using a combination of banks and retaining wall sections.

Fig. 174 Attention to detail on the embankment slopes on Pete Waterman's 'Leamington Spa', as well as the bridge, signal and lineside fence, show the level of realism that can be achieved in O-gauge.

Fig. 175   Observation of examples from the real world provides plenty of detail for modelling reference, such as the girder bridge, warning strips and hand rails on this low culvert bridge.

Fig. 176   This railway embankment sits between a river to the left and a road to the right, providing lots of ideas for modelling.

Fig. 177   With the embankment formed and the surface painted in its base colours, the surface scenic treatment can be undertaken. There is a wide variety of products on the market, including different grades and colours from the Woodland Scenics range.

Fig. 178   A base layer utilizing a blended mix of colours is a useful starting point; blends can be bought ready mixed or you can make your own.

EMBANKMENT SLOPE ANGLES

The angle of slope of an embankment in the real world is governed by the type of material, such as clay, gravel or fragmented rock, used to construct it. Specifically, the angle of slope is determined by the engineering properties in respect of the angle of repose, or, to put it more simply, the angle at which the material can be safely piled up so that it will not fail and collapse. Typically, the angle of slope will be about forty-five degrees or shallower for a stable slope.

However, where vegetation has been allowed to develop or purposely planted, steeper slope angles can be constructed and maintained stable, as the roots of the vegetation help bind the materials together. In the last thirty years or so, engineers have achieved the same effect through the increasing use of specialist geosynthetic materials, often in the form of a plastic mesh or grid. These synthetic materials act in a similar way to vegetation root systems to strengthen and stabilize

Fig. 179   Slope angles on the approach embankments to this viaduct on the Settle to Carlisle route are relatively shallow and populated with established vegetation.

Fig. 180   On this section of the coastal route east of Teignmouth, Devon, the slope angles on the cutting are much steeper, reflecting the underlying rock formations.

Fig. 181 Use of realistic slope angles on my 'Llanfair & Meifod' OO-gauge layout enhances the overall impression.

Fig. 182 On this OO9 micro-layout ('Gylchfan'), which had restricted space, retaining walls were necessary to support the embankment slopes and track bed and give the impression of a railway cut into the landscape.

the slope, thus allowing steeper angles to be safely constructed.

To make the railway infrastructure look realistic on a model railway, it is important to get the angles of the embankment slopes to look real. This will help greatly with the overall effect of the railway in the landscape. It is useful to research photographs of railway lines or simply to visit sites – always ensuring that this is done safely and without trespassing on railway land – to observe the shapes and angles of the slopes of the embankments.

Your research will give you a feel for how the slopes on your model railway layout should look to make them realistic. You will need to apply it when planning your layout, to work out how much space you have to allow, with sufficient clearances, to accommodate this type of structure. If the space available on your layout is limited, you can look at engineering structures such as retaining walls instead of embankment slopes (see Chapter 5). A retaining wall can help reduce the footprint of the embankment, as well as provide the necessary support to the railway infrastructure.

DRAINAGE

When looking at a railway embankment, it should be possible to identify some of the important features that were incorporated on all structures by the engineers, to ensure that the embankment remained stable.

Issues of ground stability below the route of an embankment were normally addressed by the installation of drainage channels at the toe of the embankment slope, to lower the water level in the soils and ensure the ground below the embankment remained drained and stable. Similarly, to ensure that the materials used to form the track bed remained stable, engineers would sometimes instal drainage channels at track-bed level, depending on the location. These would catch water falling on the track bed or water running off the embankment slopes, as well as water draining through the structure, and transport it away from the embankment slope to ensure that the structure remained stable.

Including this type of feature on your model layout will make an important contribution when you are attempting to create a realistic-looking infrastructure.

DRAINAGE AT TRACK-BED LEVEL

At the track-bed level, the running lines are raised and supported on ballast, with drainage channels often present at the margins of the track bed. Water would drain in to the channels and was normally carried to a point of discharge into a stream, river or the sea. The purpose of the drainage channel at this level was to ensure that the ballast remained drained, did not become waterlogged, and would continue to provide a firm footing for the sleepers and rails. When ballast becomes waterlogged, the material may become prone to movement and undermining, especially with the dynamic loading effect from passing trains vibrating through the waterlogged materials.

To represent this drainage system in model form on a layout, the track level should be slightly raised above the track-bed level before ballasting. For OO-gauge I tend to utilize 2mm thick polystyrene sheet. This material, intended for use as a liner on poorly finished and uneven wall surfaces prior to applying wallpaper, is available on a roll from most DIY stores. Cut it to the width of the track, plus approximately 2–4mm extra on either side of the end of the sleepers. In areas where points are to be

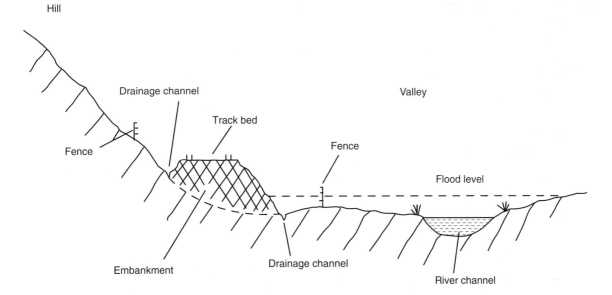

Fig. 183 Sketch cross-section to illustrate the formation of an embankment and the relative position of the drainage channels.

Fig. 184 Use of polystyrene sheet for the track bed raises the track off the baseboard, as shown on my OO-gauge 'Llanfair & Meifod' layout.

Fig. 185 Careful and neat application of ballast to the track bed enhances the realism of 'Llanfair & Meifod'.

laid, and to allow for the additional areas of ballasting seen around points, the polystyrene sheet is best cut by placing the point on the sheet first and drawing around it in soft pencil to achieve the correct shape.

The polystyrene sheet sections are fixed to the baseboard with PVA glue and the track is then glued on top of the polystyrene, also with PVA. When the PVA has dried, the track may be ballasted in the traditional manner. I prefer to apply the ballast dry using a small plastic medicine spoon and then carefully brush the ballast between the sleepers, using a trimmed piece of washing-up scrubbing pad and an

Fig. 186   Tools used for the application of ballast for a range of scales, including the scratch-built ballast applicator on the left, which is specifically for N-gauge.

Fig. 187   After application of the scenic materials, the impression of a drainage channel on 'Llanfair & Meifod' is provided by the dark-coloured 'wet' area at the margin of the track bed.

old paintbrush. The edges of the ballast are shaped with a haunch at the edge of the polystyrene, which provides the location for the drainage channel.

The representation of the channel can be as wide or narrow as you like. I tend to build up the scenery towards the track bed and stop about 10mm short of the edge of the ballasted area. The section of baseboard between the scenery and the track ballast is then painted a dark brown colour. When dry, suitable earth, soil and weed Woodland Scenics turf products are blended together and used in the

Fig. 188   Grass tufts, strips and individual long grass strands can be used to provide the impression of 'wet' drains alongside the track ballast.

normal way, to represent the area of the drainage channel. Additional details might include grass tufts and coloured scatters, to represent wild flowers.

DRAINAGE AT THE BOTTOM OF AN EMBANKMENT SLOPE

The drainage channels at the bottom of an embankment were similar to those provided at track-bed level, except that they needed to be more substantial, as the scale of the structure requiring drainage was much larger. The purpose of these drainage channels

was to ensure that the water drained through the embankment and was carried away from the structure, to ensure that the material remained stable. As with track-bed drainage, the water channels or ditches usually drained to a river or stream.

On a real railway these drainage channels or ditches may have had more than one use in terms of structural engineering. As well as being built to carry water draining from an embankment, they may have also been designed and intended to drain the land across which the railway embankment was being

Fig. 189 A more substantial drainage channel at the base of an embankment has been represented here using a culvert and water channel created on a lowered section of the baseboard.

constructed. This would have been done to ensure a firm foundation for the embankment, in particular where it was being built to cross a river valley or low-lying and poorly drained area.

A good example of this is located in Norfolk, UK, on the route of the railway line from Norwich to Great Yarmouth, via Acle. The railway line is built on an embankment across the low-lying marshes of the River Bure and River Yare valleys between Acle and Great Yarmouth. The railway line was built as a shorter, more direct route between Norwich and Great Yarmouth in the 1880s by the Great Eastern Railway.

In this example, the embankment for the railway had to be built on poorly drained marshes, in an area of high groundwater levels, which was prone to surface-water inundation. Construction of the embankment included the excavation of drainage ditches along its route, to lower groundwater by pumping the channels. The embankment was largely formed from granular materials, namely sand and gravel, but interestingly the works also included the use of bundles of wooden faggots (poles) placed on the marshes before the main fill materials were piled on top.

Representing these more substantial drainage channels at the base of the embankment in model form can offer the modeller the opportunity to create more realistic-looking engineering earthworks. Such features are often overlooked on a model railway.

On a solid baseboard surface it is possible to model these features by building up the entire ground surface above the baseboard level. The embankment can be added on top of this level and the drainage channel formed by carving out the material used to form the scenery at the bottom of the embankment. This type of approach was adopted for the construction of the OO9 micro-layout 'Gylchfan' (see Fig. 169). For this layout, the baseboard was formed from a square sheet of 9mm plywood, on to which was stuck a 25mm thick layer of polystyrene sheet. Using a craft knife (and a vacuum cleaner to remove all the loose beads of polystyrene), two sections of the polystyrene sheet were cut out, one for the culvert/stream bed at the front left-hand side and

the other for the location of a stone retaining wall at the front right-hand side of the layout (see Fig. 170).

The scenery on 'Gylchfan' was formed with polystyrene off-cuts and stiff card as formers, and scrunched-up packing paper to fill in the gaps. Once the general shape had been achieved, the whole was covered with strips of plaster bandage. Once this was set and dry, the scenery was painted in various shades of grey, brown, black and green, and then Woodland Scenics scatter materials were used to build up the layers. Noch tufts and Woodland Scenics long grasses completed the base layers, before the addition of bushes and trees from various sources.

The road up the side of the hill was formed from a zigzag piece of cardboard, cut from a large sheet then bent and stuck on risers of polystyrene to get the desired vertical alignment (see Fig. 182). All of the field walls were formed using Javis products and the section of lineside fence was from the Ratio kit. The retaining walls were formed from sheets of Wills stone, along with the Wills culvert kit (Wills ref: SS38), modified to fit the curved location on the layout. The rest of the culvert kit was used for the sides of the over-bridge on the rear left-hand side of the layout.

By way of contrast, on an open-frame baseboard the base of the channel can be shaped into the scenery profile formers, or formed by a separate piece of board to create the channel. This approach was used on my OO-gauge layout 'Llanfair & Meifod' (for more detail, see Chapter 7). In summary, I built an embankment on an open-top baseboard with a raised plywood track bed and polystyrene blocks to achieve the general land form. The base of the drainage channel or ditch was a piece of thin plywood set at the base of the embankment level. Off-cuts of timber were used to hold the base in place on the open baseboard frame.

A culvert kit from Wills (ref: SS38) was used to provide a guide to the height of the embankment and the subsequent depth of the water channel/ ditch below the rail level. With the timber formers in place, the section below the railway embankment was painted matt black to give the impression of a long culvert under the main line and adjacent yard area. The alignment of the channel was marked roughly with pencil and then the base of the channel was painted various shades of grey and brown to represent a shallow, slow-moving water channel.

TRACK CLEARANCES, GRADIENTS AND TRACK LENGTHS

For an OO-gauge layout the height required for one track to pass over another track is governed by the size of the rolling stock. On average, it is reasonable to assume a minimum of about 65mm, but it would be wise to measure the range of rolling stock intended for use on the layout to determine the actual measurement. This clearance height requirement is not related solely to the size of the rolling stock; it could be more if you plan to model overhead catenary systems. In this case, the minimum for clearance might be as much as 80mm.

When modelling N-gauge, the overhead clearance requirement will be a minimum of about 40mm. Again, however, the rolling stock will need to be checked and the height may need to be increased to about 55mm if you are considering overhead electric catenary systems on your layout.

To allow tracks to pass over one another, the optimum gradient of the line can be calculated via the usual simple test, fixing a length of track to a board and using blocks of wood to gradually raise one end. The result of this test can be used to calculate the length of embankment required to raise one track to the required height, using the following very simple formula:

$a \times \tan \varphi = b$;
where
a = the horizontal distance along the baseboard from the start of the embankment to the point at which it reaches the required clearance height;
b = the clearance height; and
φ = the optimum angle of gradient

For example, if the optimum angle of the track is found to be 3 degrees and the height required to give

clearance in OO-gauge is 65mm, then the required OO-gauge embankment will need to begin at least 1240mm from the point of crossover of the two tracks.

The length of the track bed on the embankment can be found using simple trigonometry, as it will form the hypotenuse of the triangle created by a and b. However, given the small angle of the gradient, the length will be only very slightly more than a; using the example above, this would be calculated at approximately 1242mm. To allow for inaccuracies in calculation and cutting of materials, it might be prudent to allow, say, 1250mm for the length of the embankment track bed.

Once you have tested your locomotives and worked out the gradient, you can set a general rule: for example, for every 65mm rise in level, you should allow at least 1250mm of embankment length. On this basis, for an 80mm clearance level you can work this out as a proportion of the original height (65mm) and apply this to the original length of track bed (1250mm). In this example, you would need to allow at least 1526mm, but it might be prudent to round this up to 1550mm.

The calculations above assume that the one track stays at the same level, while the other track climbs or descends to the crossover point. If a gradient is applied to both tracks, so that one track rises and the other one falls by the same amount from the starting point, then the required length of rising embankment can be halved.

ADDING SCENIC DETAILING TO EMBANKMENTS

Once you have the basic embankment formed on your layout, you can turn your attention to applying suitable detailing to it. Such features can contribute enormously to achieving a realistic finished product.

ROCK OUTCROPS
Rock outcrops can add greater variation to the sides of embankments and cuttings, and can be achieved in a number of ways.

Fig. 190 Exposed polystyrene sheet edges roughened with a file and then painted with matt enamel paints provide a cheap and effective-looking rocky outcrop on my OO-gauge 'Llanfair & Meifod' layout.

Distressed Polystyrene

Where expanded polystyrene blocks have been used to form the scenery, it is possible to leave parts of the base material exposed after applying a surface covering such as plaster bandage or filler. The exposed polystyrene surface can then be distressed by roughing up the surface with a file or rasp. Loose bits of polystyrene should be removed with a vacuum cleaner and then the remaining polystyrene block can be painted with an emulsion paint to seal it, before applying suitably coloured paints to replicate the correct type of rock. This method is good for representing rock types that are not jointed and have a rubble-like appearance on outcrops.

Rock Moulds

An alternative method that gives extremely realistic rock representations is offered by commercially available pre-cast products or by casting plaster rock in moulds such as those available from Woodland Scenics. The cast pieces of 'rock' are fixed to the embankment sides at the desired locations using impact adhesive or PVA adhesive. This method is good for the more complicated rock types that have folding, joints or layers, or a combination of these types of feature. Using these moulds enables the modeller to create as many pieces as required from a single mould. One downside to the approach is that they can add weight to the layout, which may be an important factor for a transportable layout.

Fig. 191 Selected use and placement of plaster rock moulds on this N-gauge layout enhance the mountainous scenery.
JERSEY MODEL RAILWAY CLUB

Real Rock

This method makes use of real rock materials, for example, using thin pieces of real slate to represent a rock outcrop, fixed to the scenery with impact adhesive. I used slate on my 'Llanfair & Meifod' layout at the narrow-gauge station, to represent a sheer rock face above the station. The obvious advantage of this method is that you are dealing with real rock that requires little or no preparation, except careful selection of the piece so that it fits with the setting on your layout. A big disadvantage however can be the potential to add significant weight to a layout.

Fig. 192 Real slate was used at Meifod Station on my OO-gauge 'Llanfair & Meifod' layout, to represent sheer rock outcrops.

Fig. 193 Cork was used on Tim Pollard's OO-gauge layout to model a rock face between the branch-line station on the upper level and the goods yard on the lower level.

Cork

The use of cork bark has been a traditional way of representing rock outcrops on a model railway for many years. It is a natural material and relatively lightweight. Its use seems to be less common today, possibly due to the reduced availability of cork and to the development of realistic rock moulds that can be cast as many times as required.

The cork can be broken or cut into pieces to fit the location required on a layout and can be left

Fig. 194 Shredded cork pieces, hand painted and individually glued to the layout to represent outcrops and boulders on my OO9 micro-layout 'Gylchfan'.

unpainted if preferred. However, the realism can be improved by painting or spraying with suitable rock colours and by the addition of vegetation scatter materials.

On my OO9 layout 'Gylchfan', pieces of shredded cork were used to represent large rock boulders in the bank and base of a dry river channel (*see* Fig. 194). In this instance each piece of shredded cork was painted by hand prior to fixing to the layout, using normal matt enamel paints. When dried, the pieces were fixed in place using PVA-type adhesive.

VEGETATION

As well as the use of drainage to represent real-life embankment structures, equally important is the use of vegetation and its representation on a model railway. In the real world, vegetation on embankments helps to keep moisture levels down in the soils and consequently improves the stability of the structure. However, it is clear from photographs of railway infrastructure from the late nineteenth century and early twentieth century that many of the engineering structures were relatively newly built. On these new structures, vegetation was in many places limited to grass, which seems to have been reasonably well managed.

Later photographs show that the vegetation became more established. This in part may be linked to the move from coal-fired to diesel and electric locomotives, which reduced the incidence of line-side fires from errant embers from the chimneys of passing steam trains. It might also be linked to a better understanding of the role that the vegetation could perform in terms of stabilizing embankments, as well as providing a screen to help reduce noise from the railway affecting adjacent landowners or residents.

The important point for the modeller is to look at the period being modelled, as well as the area of the country, and adjust the vegetation of the railway land on the layout accordingly. If the model seeks to represent the railways in their early development, it ought to have structures looking newly built, and the embankments should be grassed slopes with few trees and shrubs. For later periods of steam or into

Fig. 195 Studying the range of colours, variety and height of real vegetation helps when attempting to represent this feature on a model railway layout.

Fig. 196   *Grass cover in various colours, mixed with trees and bushes, provides a realistic embankment on Tim Pollard's OO-gauge layout.*

the modern era, the coverage of the lineside vegetation should be more extensive.

CULVERTS AND BRIDGES

A common feature associated with embankments is the culvert and occupation crossing, or bridge, to allow for the movement of water, people and livestock between fields and drainage channels that were often bisected by the construction of the railway. The addition of this type of structure to the layout will improve the visual representation of the scene and make the model closer to the prototype.

Kits are available to assist with recreating these types of structure, or they can be simply scratch-built from the plethora of parts and embossed plasticard available. One simple but effective kit comes from

Wills (ref: SS38), representing a culvert or cattle creep. I have used this particular kit in original and adapted form on more than one layout. On my OO-gauge layout 'Llanfair & Meifod', I made use of one of these structures for a drainage channel (see Fig. 189), and an adapted version was used on my OO9 layout 'Gylchfan', to carry the main line across a dry stream bed (see Fig. 169).

BOUNDARY MARKERS AND MILE STONES

Railway land was often marked with boundary stones indicating the limits of ownership where boundary fencing or walls may not have been needed or would have been expensive to construct. A common feature on many railways was the mile stone and

Fig. 197 A study of the details of culverts will provide useful information for the modeller.

sub-divisions of a mile indicating the distance from/to the major station on the line. It was a useful reference point when trying to locate a position for maintenance work, for example.

In model form, the representation of these types of features is less commonly covered, although castings, for example those produced by Dart Castings (ref: L19, L20 and L21), to represent mile stones, gradients and boundary stones are available. Given the relatively small size of these features and the size of the average model railway being less than a scale few hundred yards or metres long, perhaps the need to represent them on a layout is not the highest priority for the modeller!

TELEGRAPH POLES

One common feature alongside railway lines, in particular in the pre-digital technology era, would be the regular line of telegraph poles. The telegraph poles alongside the railway carried bell-code messages and telephone lines between signal boxes and stations with regards to train movements, as well as more general telephone lines. These poles would be even more evident on an embankment silhouetted against the skyline.

In model form, the poles can be easily replicated using the Ratio kits available for both N-gauge (ref: 211) and OO-gauge (ref: 452). They can be used either straight from the pack, or carefully painted

in dull matt colours to represent well-seasoned and treated timber. Picking out the insulators on the cross members in white also helps to add a certain realism.

Where telegraph poles are used on a permanent layout, it is possible in OO-gauge to add the

Fig. 198 OO-gauge telegraph poles from Ratio, appropriately painted in a dull brown, with the insulators picked out in white.

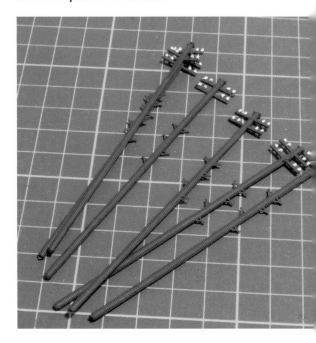

Fig. 199   Correct placement of the telegraph poles relative to the railway lines will contribute to the realism of a model, as on Pete Waterman's O-gauge layout 'Leamington Spa'.

connecting wires between poles using dark cotton thread, suitably drooping between each post and held in place with a spot of impact adhesive at each pole location. It is a painstaking task, but if carried out with a bit of patience can produce some very realistic-looking telegraph lines to enhance a layout. I have never attempted this myself, on the grounds of trying to preserve my sanity; however, there are admirable examples of this type of work on layouts such as 'Trefor', recorded in *Railway Modeller* (Halligan, 2014).

In N-gauge, the individual wires would be so fine as to make it almost impractical to represent them to actual scale. A number of N-gauge layouts have been modelled with lines, including 'Rosehill' (Keyzer and Dixon, 2014), but generally they are omitted.

On a temporary layout the problem of how to address the wires across the gaps can be an issue, although a number of sectional layouts have successfully represented the feature, including the magnificent O-gauge layout 'Long Preston' and the more recent OO-gauge layout 'Hobbs Hill' (exhibition layout), with details recorded in various articles in *Railway Modeller* over the years. The 'Hobbs Hill' layout in particular makes use of a product called 'E Z Lines' for the telegraph wires, which is essentially elastic string.

LINESIDE BUILDINGS

Along any railway route, there was a range of lineside structures, generally constructed for the use of railway maintenance teams for storage or refuge.

Fig. 200 A typical example of a lineside hut, spotted at Buckfastleigh Station – great subject matter for modelling.

The size and scale of huts were often distinct to each railway company.

For my OO-gauge layout based on a Great Western Railway theme, I built examples of the corrugated-metal lamp huts, represented by the Wills kits (ref: SS 22), as well as a corrugated pagoda building (Wills kit ref: SS 35), used as storage sheds at stations. Another example of a lineside shed is the simple timber structure typified by the OO-gauge Ratio kit (ref: 511). I have built a number of these to

Fig. 201 A corrugated-iron lineside shed, reproduced here in OO-gauge, appropriately painted and weathered for my 'Gylchfan' layout.

Fig. 202   A typical wooden platelayer's hut, positioned between the running lines by an over-bridge, provides a nice scene on Tim Pollard's OO-gauge layout.

Fig. 203   In N-gauge the structures – such as this corrugated lamp hut, ready to plant from the Graham Farish range, on my 'Duddeston Junction' layout – may be tiny and fiddly to handle, but it is worth it to add such a level of realism.

use as lineside buildings and they can also be modified for use as other useful structures for a layout, such as allotment sheds.

Similar types of structure are available for the ubiquitous concrete shed seen on Southern Railways post-1945, as represented by the Ratio kit in OO-gauge (ref: 518). Ready-to-plant structures are available from suppliers such as Bachmann (Scenecraft), for example ref: 44-169, as are resin/plaster structures requiring painting, available from suppliers such as Ten Commandments (ref: L206).

Structures are also available in N-gauge, in kit form and ready-to-plant versions. On my N-gauge layout I have used examples of the corrugated lamp huts produced by Graham Farish (Scenecraft ref: 42–114) as lineside buildings.

RUBBISH AND GRAFFITI

An increasingly common feature of modern railways, certainly on railway infrastructure over the last 50 years or so, since the mid-1960s, has been discarded rubbish and graffiti daubed across abandoned buildings, fences and in some cases rolling stock. For a model railway layout based in this later period of railway history, replicating these phenomena is a must for the sake of realism.

The modelling of detritus lying around can be achieved by using scrap bits and pieces left over from old kits, or by using some of the materials and items available from various suppliers. For example, burnt-out cars can be represented using a couple of scale cars from one of the usual suppliers suitably distressed and blackened. 'Graffiti' can be applied to buildings, fencing, walls or rolling stock as desired, either free-hand with coloured pens or using water-slide transfers, which are available in some scales.

Fig. 204   Grotty huts, old rail, a broken platelayer's trolley and other railway engineering rubbish, enhanced with grasses and creeper vegetation, all add to the atmosphere on my OO-gauge 'Llanfair & Meifod' layout.

CHAPTER FIVE

CONSTRUCTING WALLS

INTRODUCTION

Walls come in all shapes and sizes and a wide variety of material types have been used in their construction, either naturally occurring materials including wood, slate or stone worked into suitable size or shape, or man-made materials such as brick or concrete, which have been manufactured for a specific use.

In the railway environment, walls are most often utilized either as a physical boundary, such as for stations, goods yards, or property boundaries in urban areas, or as an engineering structure to protect or support the railway infrastructure. Inevitably, in some instances the same wall might perform both functions.

WALLS AS BOUNDARIES

When walls are being used as boundaries, they are constructed from a number of common types of material, and there are various ways to represent this on a model railway layout. Some worked examples are described below, using a variety of kit and scratch-build methods, both of which can be relatively easily achieved by the modeller without the need for advanced skill levels.

STONE WALLS

Naturally occurring materials such as rock used for building stone walls would have been influenced by the local geology of the area where the wall is constructed. This would have been particularly

Fig. 205 Tunnel portal wall on the coastal route west of Dawlish, which is also a retaining wall.

Fig. 206   Granite-block drystone boundary wall, typical of the pink rocks of Jersey in the Channel Islands; note the established vegetation and irregular block sizes.

Fig. 207   A dressed-stone wall as a highway boundary in Dartmoor National Park, UK.

significant in the pre-industrial era, when transport to move materials over great distances, and a suitable infrastructure to support it, would have been limited. In the eighteenth century, the transport infrastructure of Great Britain was improved by the construction of a network of canals, enabling goods to be shipped over much greater distances and distributed over wider areas. This was improved further in the early nineteenth century with the advent of the railways. By the twentieth century,

it was possible for materials quarried all over the world to be shipped to just about anywhere as part of global trade.

For the purposes of modelling UK railways, a good indicator of the regional location and period being represented can be provided by the selection of the most appropriate material to model the walls. For example, drystone limestone walls are a distinctive feature of the Cotswolds and parts of the Lincolnshire Wolds, while drystone walling formed from millstone grit is a distinctive regional feature of Yorkshire and The Dales. In other areas of the UK, granite or sandstone would be sourced locally for wall construction. In East Anglia, there is very little in the way of local stone or hard-rock geology that can be quarried for building stone. In this area there are fewer stone boundary walls, but where present the use of flint derived from the chalk is a common and very distinctive building material.

SLATE WALLS

Slate is relevant in a relatively limited area in terms of its use as a building material. The use of slate is a particular feature of structures in North Wales as well as in some parts of Cumbria. The material was widely used in slab form for walls and the roofs of buildings, as well as for the construction of boundary walls. Slate was also used as a material for fencing, in the form of thin slate sheets standing on edge and tied together with intertwined wire (see Chapter 6).

BRICK WALLS

Brick boundary walls are more common in built-up or urban areas of the country, but even with bricks there can be a variation in colour and size, reflecting regional differences. In parts of central and eastern England, for example, the bricks used were a yellowish-brown colour. The most common form in the country is the red brick, but even within that range, there are variations in terms of size and colour.

The colour variations in brick production are reflective of the colour of the local clay soils that were used in the localized brick industries around the country. Size variation was also down to the individual brick producer, before a standard size was adopted by the industry.

Other colour variations of brick, notably blue and black, can be seen providing decorative patterning in many buildings, particularly of the Victorian period. Blue bricks also served a purpose as engineering bricks, for structures where there was a need for more hard-wearing materials.

Moving into the late nineteenth and early twentieth century, the variation in size and colour of bricks diminished. Brick manufacturing became more industrialized and larger in scale, so that many of the smaller producers disappeared. The end product became more standardized, and more uniform in size, colour and quality.

TIMBER WALLS

Timber has been used for centuries to form walls in buildings, but in terms of infrastructure its use is less common. The most obvious example of timber being used on the railways is seen in the low retaining walls formed from railway sleepers than can often be observed in cuttings or on low embankments. This suggests that the concept of recycling is not a new phenomenon confined to the modern world. Another example of the use of timber is in the construction of cribs, a type of retaining structure. As with the previous example these uses of timber relate more to engineering walls than to boundary structures.

PRE-CAST CONCRETE WALLS

In the early twentieth century the use of pre-cast concrete became more popular and widespread as a building method, following developments in the techniques used in its manufacture. At the quality and robustness of the product improved, pre-cast concrete beams and posts began to be used to form walls and fences (see also Chapter 6).

In the UK, the Southern Railway in particular was associated with the widespread use of this type of material for a range of building and infrastructure projects. Its use was much in evidence in the investment and improvements carried out by the Southern Railway after the Grouping of 1923. It was a new medium of construction that enabled designers to create a modern and distinctive style of railway architecture, with 1920s and 30s Art Deco styling.

WALLS AS ENGINEERING STRUCTURES

As well as the role of defining boundaries, walls were and still are often used as engineering structures, to protect or support railway infrastructure in a rural

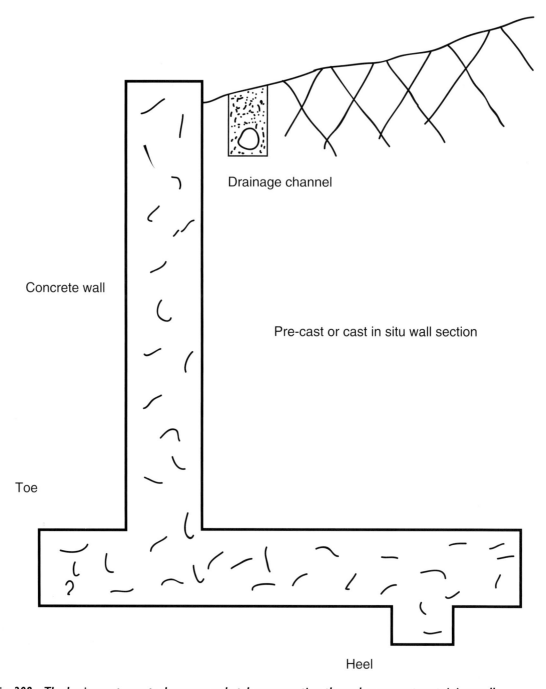

Fig. 208 *The basic components shown on a sketch cross-section through a concrete retaining wall.*

or an urban setting. In a railway environment, there are wing walls to tunnels and bridges, and retaining walls, either to support a railway line or to protect it from land through which the line passes in a cutting.

In the modern era, when there is more understanding of the need to mitigate the environmental impacts of railway infrastructure, walls have also been used as noise barriers.

Fig. 209   Concrete retaining walls alongside a busy suburban railway, near Warrington, UK; note the weathering and the established vegetation.

RETAINING WALLS

The use of retaining walls by railway engineers was and still is a fundamental part of the railway design process. A retaining wall can be used to limit the extent of excavation for cuttings, as well as to provide support to slopes where ground conditions will not allow normal earthwork slope cuttings and embankments. A further use of retaining walls, in particular in urban areas, is where space is limited to accommodate the railway.

Where retaining walls have been used in cuttings, it is often the case that the original railway cutting or embankment may have been built to accommodate one or two running lines. However, as the railway networks and traffic levels have grown, space has been less readily available for expansion into more running lines. Retaining walls allowed the railway engineers to construct additional railway lines within the original land boundary, without compromising the stability of the cutting or the embankment slopes.

Retaining walls can be formed from a wide variety of materials and the choice was usually determined by what was most readily available locally. In North America, for example, the plentiful supply of wood for timber structures provided a much quicker and easier source of raw materials than quarrying rock. As a result, timber retaining structures, as well as tunnel portals, culverts and trestle bridges, were all common features in nineteenth-century railway development in North America.

By contrast, in the UK, where large wooded areas were not always available, railway engineers made much greater use of brick and locally quarried stone to construct retaining walls. This practice gave a regional flavour to the structures, as it did in the construction of boundary walls too. In certain special circumstances, the engineer may have imported stone from a quarry outside the local area, in order to create an impressive structure that would make a statement of intent for the railway company. An example of this might be Brunel's grand wing walls and portal at the English or eastern entrance to the Severn Tunnel. These were built using limestone blocks, transported at some expense to the location,

Fig. 210 Stone retaining wall at Teignmouth Station, Devon, where the railway squeezes through the town.

Fig. 211 Concrete retaining wall between the ring road and the railway platform at Teignmouth Station.

creating a grand structure befitting what was a major engineering achievement of its time.

In urban areas, retaining walls were often needed to support ground around the railway infrastructure. In these instances, the walls were used either to support land built up for railway development, or, more commonly, to provide support to the ground beyond the railway boundary. In the latter case, the use of retaining walls was the result of simple economics – using earth embankments or cuttings for the railways would take up more space in an area where land value was at a premium. Urban railways are therefore often characterized by brick-walled embankments and viaducts threading through the

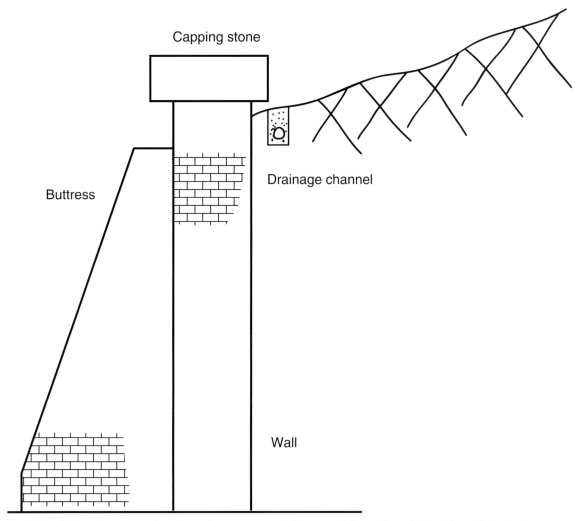

Capping stone

Buttress

Drainage channel

Wall

Fig. 212   A sketch cross-section through a masonry retaining wall shows the relationship with the buttresses.

development, with all sorts of land uses in the space below the railway.

In rural areas, where railways cut through areas of higher ground, brick retaining walls were often used to reduce the land take of the railway. This would also reduce the impact of the railway on the existing landscape or any planned future development.

Retaining walls have a number of features that are worth modelling to ensure that a model provides a realistic interpretation of the real thing. Typically, certain sections of retaining wall will also include a number of buttresses at regular intervals, to provide additional support to the structure. The size and

regularity of the buttress constructions was usually determined by an assessment of the height of the retaining wall required and the ground conditions at the site.

Another common feature of railway retaining walls is the alcoves at regular intervals alongside the tracks. These refuges were intended, and are still used, to provide shelter for maintenance gangs working on the tracks, as they allow trains to pass. When adding retaining walls to a model railway layout, these are the sort of features and details that need to be considered, to make the model a more believable representation of the real world.

In the twentieth century, the use of brick and stone for engineering features was largely replaced by the use of concrete, either as pre-cast units or mass structures cast in situ. In the twenty-first century, the use of concrete is all but exclusive in the formation of large civil-engineering structures such as retaining walls.

CRIB WALLS

One engineering structure that is used as a retaining wall on highways, and to a degree on railway infrastructure, is the crib wall. This type of structure is an open lattice of interlocking beams and uprights that is used to provide support to a low embankment or cutting face. Historically, this type of structure was typically formed from timber, but more modern construction techniques utilize pre-cast concrete or composite material beams in place of timber, increasing the potential longevity of the structure. In the model environment, such structures are more likely to be relevant to layouts representing more modern prototypes.

WING WALLS

Wing walls are usually associated with a bridge or tunnel either over or under the railway and can be formed from a variety of materials. Most commonly, steam-era structures of this type would be built of brick or stone, whereas concrete is more likely to be the relevant material when looking at railways of the modern era.

The purpose of the wing wall was to provide support to the cutting or embankment slopes around the tunnel or bridge portal, and to help prevent the collapse of material on to the running lines. In early railway development, the wing walls to tunnel portals formed part of the 'frame' for the portal and were generally constructed from the same stone as the portal. They often also carried the same decorative stonework.

NOISE BARRIERS

The noise barrier is a more recent type of structure, as engineers building highways or railways have been required to reduce the environmental impact of the

Fig. 213 Heavy staining on the wing walls, from water running off the retained hillside above the railway, provides interesting detail for modellers; the half arch is a result of the tunnel-mouth extension when the track was doubled, and provides support to the portal wall.

transport infrastructure on neighbouring land uses, particularly in urban areas. As with walls, the materials used for the construction of these structures can vary, but there are often requirements to use them sympathetic to the local environment.

The use of timber panelling and concrete is a common method, but a more unusual prototype is the glass or polycarbonate sheeting seen in Europe alongside road and rail routes. The advantage of this is that it minimizes noise but also allows light through. In terms of railway modelling, this type of screening could be replicated using clear plasticard sheets, suitably coloured and shaped to match the profiles of the prototype.

BLAST WALLS

Blast walls are not commonly seen, either in the real world or in model form. However, the information might be relevant for anyone considering modelling one of the numerous temporary railway lines and depots that were created during the Second World War, or a freelance design based on this subject matter.

As the name suggests, a blast wall was intended to provide protection against blast damage. Given the period from which many of these features date, a combination of brick, concrete and earth embankments needs to be considered. In the context of a model railway layout, these walls can be constructed in a similar fashion to other retaining walls or boundary walls, but they should be positioned to protect entry points to key buildings and structures such as bunkers or storage sheds.

SOURCES OF WALLS FOR MODEL RAILWAYS

When constructing walls for a model railway layout there are many suitable sources, from ready-to-plant structures to raw materials that may be used for scratch-building.

READY-TO-PLANT STRUCTURES

A number of manufacturers, including Hornby Skaledale and Javis, produce ready-formed sections

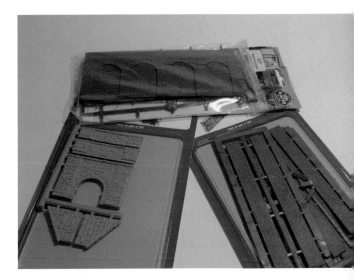

Fig. 214   Various wall styles are available in OO-gauge kits.

Fig. 215   A simple but effective granite stone wall produced by Javis Scenics, using grey foam strip on to which granite chippings have been stuck with glue.

of wall in OO-gauge that are painted and in some cases weathered, ready for the modeller to instal on their layout. Hornby produces 'Limestone' and 'Granite' drystone wall sections, which are available

Fig. 216   Ready-to-plant Hornby Skaledale wall products, repainted and weathered, in use on my OO-gauge layout 'Llanfair & Meifod'.

as straight or curved sections, with other special sections for right-angle corners, gates and stiles. There are even sections of broken-down walling available, in case that is an appropriate feature on a layout.

A similar range of products is available in N-gauge, although these are often produced as the cast sections only and require the modeller to paint them in the colours to match the rock of the region where the layout is set. The N-gauge wall sections may be obtained direct from an eBay retailer and are supplied rough-cast, requiring some preparation work before painting and using on a layout. The plaster castings are soft enough to be easily cleaned up with

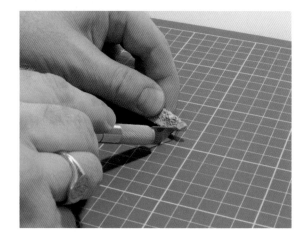

Fig. 218   Wall castings are of variable quality and some require trimming of the joints with a sharp craft knife.

Fig. 217   Cast-stone wall sections for N-gauge are available from a number of suppliers; they require painting before use.

a sharp craft knife, taking care not to break the delicate mouldings, which are very small. When each section has been cleaned up, it can be painted either prior to fixing to the layout or after fixing. The best way to attach these wall sections to a layout is with PVA-type adhesive or impact adhesive.

The sections of wall, both OO-gauge and N-gauge, come with alternative upper or lower stepped ends so that the sections join together and do not leave a vertical joint.

I have made extensive use of the Hornby Skaledale product range of wall sections for my OO-gauge

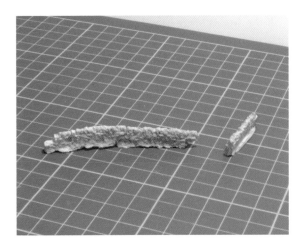

Fig. 219 Wall sections trimmed and cleaned up ready for painting.

Fig. 221 Keep a selection of acrylic paints handy for various modelling requirements; small tubes are better value and can be replenished easily.

Fig. 220 The castings can be painted with acrylic or enamel paints: start with a matt enamel base colour and then use the acrylics dry-brushed for enhancing colours and weathering.

layout. As supplied, the colour represented a pale limestone-type wall, which was not representative for the area of the Welsh Marches where my layout is notionally, albeit fictionally, located. This was easily modified, however, with a mix of acrylic paints being used to replicate the darker stone of the region.

The sections of wall were all painted before being used on the layout, to achieve a more uniform appearance. The use of acrylic paints allowed some of the underlying paint and weathering to show through and this was augmented as required by further dry-brush weathering of the wall sections.

When dry, the wall sections were then loosely arranged on the layout to check alignments, locations of joints and the need or otherwise to alter the scenery to accommodate the wall sections. For more information on fixing and building the walls on a layout, see later.

KIT-BUILT WALLS

There is a range of kits to build walls available in OO-gauge and N-gauge from a number of suppliers, including plastic kits from Ratio and Wills and card kits from Metcalfe. These kits allow the modeller to cut and adapt the wall sections to fit the locations on the layout where they are needed, but require more work from the modeller in terms of building and painting than do the ready-to-plant structures.

For a dressed-stone wall in OO-gauge, the Wills kit (ref: SS36) is a good place to start. This kit provides parts to construct a wall approximately 520mm long, made up of four sections of approximately 130mm in length, with dressed-stone facing to both sides

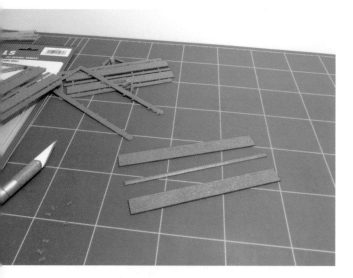

Fig. 222 The dressed-stone wall kit from Wills comprises four sprues, each with two wall sections embossed on one side and a length of capping stones.

of the wall. Each wall section also includes a length of capping stones as a ridge to the wall, as well as a number of similarly moulded pieces for corners, joints or wall ends.

Fig. 223 The wall sections are glued together smooth side to smooth side using liquid polystyrene cement and then the capping stone moulding is cut to fit.

If the wall is being used in a location where only one side is visible, then it is possible effectively to double the length of the dressed wall facing the viewer. To provide capping to the extended wall, a suitable capping stone strip will need to be sourced from another kit or a suitable alternative fabricated from scratch using scored plasticard. It might also be possible with careful cutting lengthwise of the capping stone strips supplied in the kit to provide sufficient capping for the full length of wall.

SCRATCH-BUILT WALLS

The option to scratch-build walls provides the modeller with the opportunity to recreate a specific style or size of wall. Scratch-building is probably going to be a requirement where the layout represents a real location, as the materials available as kits or ready-to-plant items are unlikely to be exactly right. There are a couple of potential options for scratch-building described here, with more detailed descriptions of actual projects given later.

I have used plastic, card and thin plywood for scratch-building walls on the layouts that I have created over the years. The suitability of each medium depends on what the wall is for and the size of the structure required. On my N-gauge layout, for example, both plastic and card were used to construct various wall sections. Embossed-stone plasticard sheets were used to form the basis of a cutting retaining wall, with heavy-duty card cut, suitably scored and painted to represent capping stones to the wall and buttresses. Brick paper mounted on card was used to form the garden boundary walls of the terraced cottages, with gates from the Ratio concrete panel fence kit (*see* Chapter 6) providing access to the garden.

For an urban scene on a club N-gauge layout, we used thin 4mm plywood to create a long retaining wall behind the main station of the layout. Once the basic structure was formed, I then used brick paper printed on to heavy card as an overlay to the plywood wall. Buttresses formed in the same manner on card were then cut and used to hide the joints between the card sections. Capping stones for the wall were also formed from heavy-duty card

Fig. 224   Sheets of embossed-stone plasticard were used to create the railway-cutting retaining wall, with one section cut into vertical strips to form the buttresses and thick card scored for the capping stones.

Fig. 225   Red-brick garden walls for these cottages in N-gauge were formed from thick card covered in brick paper scanned and printed from the PC.

Fig. 226   The same method was used for the brick retaining walls to the rear of the goods yard.

suitably painted and scored before fixing along the top of the wall.

PAINTING AND WEATHERING

Once the walls have been built, the next step in making them look realistic is to apply a suitable coat of paint as a base colour and then as required to add weathering detail. Although ready-to-plant structures do come pre-painted, the colour schemes and the final finish on the model often still require some work to improve the finished appearance.

Ready-to-plant structures generally require at least some form of light weathering to tone down brighter colours or to take the sheen of surfaces and make them appear duller and, therefore, more realistic. For plastic kits, while the colour of the plastic in the moulding may be reasonable, a coat of paint or a wash of diluted enamel paint will dull the appearance of the plastic and make it look more natural.

Fig. 227   Section of embossed-stone plasticard painted with matt enamel grey base coat and then dry-brushed with acrylics, to replicate the features and weathering inspired by photographs of real walls.

BUILDING WALLS FOR MODEL RAILWAYS

Fig. 228   Ready-to-plant dressed-stone walls used here with buildings to form a timber merchant's yard on Tim Pollard's OO-gauge layout.

Fig. 229   Ready-to-plant rough-stone walling used on a farm scene on Tim Pollard's OO-gauge layout.

ADDING READY-TO-PLANT WALLS TO THE LANDSCAPE

There are a number of suppliers of resin-cast ready-to-plant wall structures, including Hornby, which produces the Skaledale wall system in OO-gauge. Installing the Skaledale OO-gauge wall system on a layout can be quickly accomplished by setting out the wall sections straight from the packet. Each piece has a stepped end so that it fits over or under the accompanying piece. If you are planning to set the layout and the wall on a flat baseboard area, then the wall sections can be laid out as required to achieve

Fig. 230   Sections of the ready-to-plant walls used for field boundaries, set into the polystyrene landscape surface, provide a realistic scene on my OO-gauge 'Llanfair & Meifod' layout.

Fig. 231 Lengths of broken-down wall, bushes, trees and long grasses all give the impression of a run-down and unused area of rough ground on 'Llanfair & Meifod'.

the wall arrangement for the location. They can be held in place temporarily with a spot of Blu Tack or similar.

For a more permanent layout, the wall sections can be simply held in place with PVA glue or impact adhesive. Once the adhesive has set, the joints between the sections can be touched up with a thin veneer of filler, to hide the joint lines and to disguise any gaps where there might not be a perfect match between adjacent wall sections.

Using the walling on undulating scenery requires a little more preparatory work along the proposed alignment of the wall, as indeed would be the case in the real world. The resin pieces of wall section come in fixed lengths, which may be of varying size and shape, but they will not flex to follow the curvature of a landscape. In this instance, you will need to create a reasonably flat base on which to fix the sections.

Based on my experience, installation of the walls is best achieved by creating the scenery first and then making the wall fit the scenery. Once the basic ground contours of the scenery have been created, using plaster-impregnated bandage over polystyrene blocks, this is left to harden off. The alignment of the wall is then marked using a pencil and the wall sec-

tions roughly placed to see what works best for the location. Once the appropriate wall sections have been selected, use each section in its intended location to mark the plan outline, as well as the width of the wall, on to the scenery surface.

Using a heavy duty craft knife, cut the surface plaster bandage layer and carefully remove sufficient polystyrene packing material below to create a relatively flat base on which the wall sections can sit. Importantly, the base area does not have to be perfectly flat, as any small undulations can be accommodated later with adhesive and/or disguised with filler once the wall has been fixed in position. Before fixing any of the wall sections in place, complete the cutting of the scenery as necessary for the length of wall being installed and then trial-fit the wall sections, checking alignment and fit, before fixing permanently.

When you are happy with the setting out, start at one end of the wall or at a corner section and work along, fixing each wall section in place to the underlying scenery with an appropriate adhesive such as PVA, or an impact adhesive that will not melt the polystyrene. You may need to weight each section of wall down until the glue has set, to hold it in position.

Fig. 232 Joints and gaps in the walls are filled and suitably scribed to match the walls, then painted and weathered to blend in.

Fig. 233 This section of wall ends right at the front of the layout, but was disguised by use of filler, painting, weathering and placement of vegetation and a rickety shed for the sheep.

When the wall sections have set in position, use a cheap filler (for example, a tube of Polyfilla) to fill any gaps between the wall sections and the adjacent ground surface of the scenery, as well as any gaps in the wall joints. Before the filler has dried off, use a scalpel to scribe the filler to match the stonework of the resin sections. Where the gaps extend to the top edge of the wall sections, you can also attempt to shape the top edge of the filler and scribe it to match adjacent wall sections. This completes the installation of the wall. Where necessary, all that remains to be done is painting over the filler to match the rest of the wall, using a mix of enamel and acrylic paints.

CONSTRUCTING STONE RETAINING WALLS WITH EMBOSSED PLASTICARD

The guidance given here, on the construction of a retaining wall using commercially available embossed plasticard sheets, is for an N-gauge layout, but the methods and principles remain the same for other smaller or larger scales.

My plan was to create an urban-themed layout, to maximize the use of a limited baseboard area and to create a usable area on two levels for operational railways. The layout was inspired by similar examples described in a number of articles in *Railway Modeller*. In urban areas, railway infrastructure had to be threaded through or below existing development and constructed to minimize the land take.

Fig. 234 A good example of a stone retaining wall in O-gauge, on 'Leamington Spa' by Pete Waterman; from viewing distance, it looks extremely realistic.

Fig. 235 A low retaining wall formed from Wills dressed-stone sheets provides a corner scene on this OO9 micro-layout.

Fig. 236   High-level view of my N-gauge 'Duddeston Junction' layout, showing the various retaining walls and boundary walls.

Replicating this in model form would require the construction of a retaining wall between the upper-level yard area and the lower level through line and redundant junction.

The premise behind this N-gauge layout was that the upper level represented an urban industrial setting, with factory sidings and small subsidiary goods yard facility, including a fuel depot, served by an industrial tramway. This allowed for the use of less stringent track construction, with no signalling, small radius points and sharp curves, with the track weaving its way through the industrial area.

The lower-level track was meant to represent a secondary route, used primarily for freight workings and the odd local passenger workings, with the opportunity for the occasional diverted main-line service during engineering possessions. The lower level would also include an abandoned and partially lifted junction, which provided the name for the layout, 'Duddeston Junction', as displayed on the disused signal box at the junction. Overall, the intention was to create a layout representing the 1960s transition steam to diesel period, with an air of neglect and lack of infrastructure investment.

Fig. 237 A retaining wall with a low embankment, topped by a timber post and rail fence, adds depth to the scenery on 'Duddeston Junction', between the lower railway level and the central goods yard access road.

The retaining walls were constructed using packs of embossed plasticard sheets from Peco (ref: NB-40); each pack contains four sheets of dressed-stone walling and the height of the individual sheets, at about 63mm, set the height of the retaining wall to the upper level of the layout. This was purely to make the project easier, obviating the need to cut and join sheets together vertically.

The upper level of the layout was constructed using expanded polystyrene blocks to support a 'baseboard 'of heavy-duty artist's mounting card, approximately 2mm thick. The use of this type of thick card represented a compromise between providing a reasonably sturdy base on which to lay the tramway and industrial sidings and keeping the overall weight of the layout down. While this would work for N-gauge, for OO-gauge a thicker card or, more likely, thin plywood (say, 4mm thick) would be required for the track bed to ensure that the track would be usable long-term.

The wall sections were painted before being applied to the layout. Painting of the sheets started with a mid-grey enamel base colour, followed by dry brushing with a range of acrylic paints until the desired effect had been achieved (see Fig. 227). One section of the embossed plasticard was cut vertically into strips approximately 15mm wide to represent the buttresses for the wall. The buttresses were spaced and fixed to the wall at the junction of individual sheets to hide the vertical joints (see Fig. 233).

The painted sections of wall were then fixed to the layout with impact adhesive. Glue was applied along the bottom edge of the sheets to fix to the lower-level baseboard and also along the edge of the upper-level baseboard, to which the wall sections were then fixed. To instal the wall, I began with the tunnel mouth over the lower-level track at the right-hand side of the layout (as viewed from the front). I then worked my way along the cutting, fixing the sheets only when the previous one had set reasonably firmly, so that it was not dislodged while positioning the next one.

Once all of the wall sections had been fixed in position, they were left overnight to allow the adhesive to set, before adding the buttress strips over each joint. These were also fixed using impact adhesive. When all of the sections had been fixed and set, the paintwork was touched up as required to hide any adhesive that might have seeped through joints or at the base of the wall.

To complete the feature, a row of capping stones was required for the top of the wall and buttresses.

More of the thick artist's card was cut in to strips, to the width of the plasticard sheet, plus an overlap of about 0.5mm. Each of the strips was then scored using a small flat-head screwdriver, to represent individual stones. Scoring of the capping stones was achieved by marking the strip by eye with a pencil and then lightly scoring along each pencil mark with the same small flat-head screwdriver.

Marking out the capping stones without measuring gives stones of approximately the same size, but sufficiently random to appear natural. The capping stone strips were then painted using an appropriate pale grey enamel paint, contrasting with the wall colouring. When dry, the strips of stones were fixed to the top of the wall with impact adhesive. The capping stones for the buttresses were cut slightly larger to stand out from the wall capping stones.

CONSTRUCTING SCRATCH-BUILT BRICK RETAINING WALLS

Brick was also a common material type for the construction of retaining walls and these can be reproduced for use in a layout, either with embossed plasticard or printed brick paper sheets. Printed sheets can also be applied to building stone walls for a layout.

Another example constructed for the same N-gauge layout was the brick retaining wall used at the rear of the factories and goods yard on the upper level. (As with the stone walls, although this example was for an N-gauge layout, the same methods and principles can be applied to other scales and gauges.) On this N-gauge layout the brick retaining wall served a number of purposes. It screened the section of the tramway along the rear of the upper level of the layout and the small fiddle yard (see Fig. 226). It also hid the connection between the upper-level loop and the industrial siding complex and goods yard in the centre of the layout's upper level.

The wall also provided a scenic break at the rear of the industrial area and allowed a further higher-level section of scenery to be built, including a road with further factory buildings. This step up in the scenery gave a greater apparent depth to the layout and helped disguise the rear sections of the loop and exchange sidings on the lower level of the layout.

The brick wall sections were formed by scanning a blank wall section from one of the card kits and then printing this out to form a brick paper sheet. The brick paper was then glued with PVA on to 2mm thick card, such as artist's card, and then left to dry. Once it had dried, the wall height was measured and

Fig. 238 'Newcastle' by Tim Pollard: a rising embankment in OO-gauge for the road and tram tracks utilizes a stone retaining wall.

Fig. 239 To accommodate the signal box at the north end of the main station on 'Newcastle', the embankment has been excavated and a stone retaining wall constructed.

marked with a pencil and then the card was cut to the required height. The wall was cut into sections to give sufficient height so that the upper scenic layer allowed enough headroom over the tramway track, and then approximately 8mm was added to provide a low wall above the planned road level.

One section of the cut wall was divided into vertical strips approximately 15mm wide to be used as buttresses (as on the stone walls) for the stone retaining wall to the railway cutting. All of the wall sections and buttresses were then painted along all of the cut edges, using a brick-red colour mixed

Fig. 240 Fabricating the red-brick retaining walls for my N-gauge layout, and for the rebuild of the main station on the local club layout, from 2mm thick card covered with homemade brick paper scanned and printed from the PC.

Fig. 241 Buttresses formed by cutting one of the larger sections into short strips; the edges of the card were painted with acrylic paints colour-matched to the brick paper.

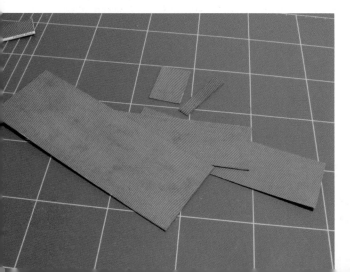

Fig. 242   Angled retaining wall supporting land to the rear of the cottages on my 'Duddeston Junction' layout; in the foreground, Duddeston Model Railway club have taken ownership of one of the old storage sheds!

from acrylic paints to match the brick paper. This helped hide any white, or other colour, base card at joints and also meant that the top edge could be left without capping stones

The wall sections were added to the layout only after all of the track had been laid and ballasted where required, and not before the wire-in tube point control rodding had been installed and checked. Off-cuts of card were used to support the wall and also to support the card base for the road level above, as this was added at the same time as the wall. The buttresses were added once the wall sections had set in place.

At the right-hand end of the layout (when viewed from the front), adjacent to the area where the row of cottages was placed, the retaining wall was cut to angle down to follow the proposed ground contours. In addition, when fitting this wall section, the wall was angled away from the vertical by about 10 degrees. This was done to create an impression of depth to the scenery and also helped to achieve a more realistic-looking section of wall, rather than a

vertical piece that just suddenly stopped at this point. The surface contours were formed around the wall using plaster bandage, and the final result was really quite effective.

The wall was finished off by a section of barrier fence around the curve in the road and opposite the road junction, representing highway safety fencing. The sections were taken from the Ratio trestle bridge and turntable kits (see Fig. 237). The bridge had been built for use on the American-themed layout 'Pine Ridge Creek' at my local model railway club, but the fence sections had been deemed surplus to requirements. They were painted a suitable dull grey colour and then fixed with impact adhesive to the top edge of the card wall sections.

INSTALLING SCRATCH-BUILT GARDEN WALLS

The cottages on my N-gauge layout needed brick garden walls. These could have been formed using brick paper mounted on thick card, as for the retaining walls, but for my layout I had enough leftover sections from the sheets used to create the retaining walls (see Fig. 225). These off-cuts were measured and cut as required to give a scale height of about five feet. The edges of the wall sections were then painted with acrylic paints to match the brick colour, and the walls were fixed in place after the buildings had been fixed in position.

The gates to the rear gardens came from the Ratio concrete fence kits (see Chapter 6), and were held in place with impact adhesive along the base and the hinged side to the adjacent wall section.

Fig. 243 Retaining walls to the rear of the goods yard and factories on 'Duddeston Junction', supporting the road and other industrial buildings beyond.

CHAPTER SIX

INSTALLING FENCES

DIFFERENT TYPES OF FENCING

There are many different types of fence, in terms of style, size and construction materials. Fences were used in the railway environment specifically in order to enclose railway land and prevent access, either by accident or deliberate action. The aim was not only to protect the railway infrastructure, but also to protect the public from the danger of moving trains.

Typical materials used to construct fences comprise wood, concrete and various metals, and the use of specifically local materials, for example, slate

Fig. 244 The fencing between the railway and the highways to prevent access on this suburban railway in Lisbon, Portugal, is somewhat limited.

Fig. 245 At Dawlish in Devon, the lineside fencing varies from steel palisade on the right to the more retro period metal railings on the left.

Fig. 246 Numerous fence types, from traditional timber to modern chain-link, at Buckfastleigh Station.

slabs in certain parts of North Wales, was a common practice in the nineteenth and early twentieth centuries. In more recent times, man-made composite materials have come into their own. With the multitude of railway companies involved in developing and operating the rail network over the decades, there is a wide variety of fence types to be seen, with some regional styles evident.

The most common type of boundary fence for the railways during its early development was comprised of wooden, later concrete, posts with galvanized wire. When the casting of concrete became widespread as a construction technique in the early twentieth century, the Southern Railway, formed out of the 1923 Grouping, was a significant user of this material for fencing posts and panels. (It also put

Fig. 247 Metal security lineside fencing is evident here, even in what appears to be an inaccessible railway cutting, near Warrington, UK.

Fig. 248 A low-level metal chain-link fence and hedging give the approach to Oss Station in the Netherlands a more welcoming and attractive appearance than that normally associated with modern railway infrastructure

the material to many other engineering and building uses, for example, in constructing platforms and line-side huts.) Further details on the use of engineering concrete for a wide variety of uses by the Southern Railway are provided in B.K. Cooper's handbook (1983).

In urban areas, railway fences tended to be more robust, especially in more modern times, to prevent trespass and vandalism of the infrastructure and rolling stock. Chain-link mesh fencing was one commonly used type, although it has been increasingly superseded by Weldmesh, or heavy-duty metal

Fig. 249 Heavily weathered and rusting metal platform fencing on the seaward side of Dawlish Station, Devon, gives a clue to the site's exposure to south-westerly gales and heavy seas!

Fig. 250 Further to the east at Dawlish Station, the platform fencing is formed from heavy-duty timber and, despite the weathering, seems to be in a better condition than the metal fencing.

palisade fencing. Beyond the railway boundary, fences have many uses.

It is important when modelling a railway in a landscape to include fencing as part of the scenery, where appropriate. All sorts of fences can be used on model railway layouts to represent the real world. A number of different types of fencing, from the early steam age to the modern period, are described here, along with guidance on how to incorporate them into a layout, and hints and tips on installation.

When planning a layout, it is helpful to think about how the railway fits into the landscape, whether the setting is rural or urban, and how the boundaries of the railway land as well as other land uses will be defined. The modeller needs to consider where the fence lines might be located; the materials from which they are they are likely to be constructed; and how they might be installed.

Reference to illustrated books, with old photographs of landscapes and railway lines, will help in this regard. Extensive research might seem a bit unnecessary, but old photographs are a good source of inspiration and allow the modeller to get a feel for what might and might not be appropriate on a model railway, given its period, region or setting. In addition, a visit to the actual area will help greatly with identifying real-world examples that can be recreated in model form.

As with walls, fencing in the real world follows the ground contours, and it should do the same on a model railway layout, in this case following the ground profile created by the modeller. In practical terms, the fence posts should be progressively installed along the fence alignment. It is best to start with a small section and work your way along the line of the fence a short piece at a time. Do not be tempted to try to do too much in one modelling session, as you are likely to encounter issues with keeping the fence vertical. This may or may not prove to be a problem, depending on what you are modelling.

Furthermore, where the ground profile of the scenery is undulating, it is advisable to let the glue set before changing direction laterally and vertically. It is also a good idea to use small blocks of wood, the handle of a knife or other small tool, or in fact anything suitably sized, to hold the fence upright and fixed to the ground until the glue has set.

One thing to consider when modelling fences is to try to replicate the styles that were prototypical to the region and/or period being modelled. For example, if you are modelling a 1920s or 30s steam-age branch line, palisade fencing or security chain-link fencing would not be prototypical or appropriate. Researching old photographs, sketches and drawings for this kind of detail will guide the modeller

Fig. 251   A field-boundary wall and two-strand barbed wire fence provide a simple but effective stock-proof barrier, Dartmoor National Park, Devon.

Fig. 252   This post and rail fence on 'Llanfair & Meifod' has been formed around the area of rough ground and has become intertwined with vegetation.

towards the right styles and types of fencing. This will help you to create the overall impression and feel for the prototype being modelled, even if the layout is not based on any particular real location. For the average railway modeller, the aim is usually to create a believable general representation of a period and region.

POST AND WIRE

One common type of boundary fence that would be appropriate for both steam-age and modern diesel/electric traction is the post and wire, comprising either timber, metal or concrete posts with a number of wire stands threaded through pre-drilled holes. In OO-gauge, kits for this type of fencing are available from suppliers such as Ratio (Ratio ref: 423), and a relatively quick and simple installation process will result in an extremely realistic lineside feature. The instructions with the kit are straightforward – the main skill of the modeller will lie in being patient enough to allow the posts to set and not to do too much at a time.

The instructions for the OO-gauge kit recommend that a fence post should be installed for approximately each 20mm-length of fencing, but this is at the discretion of the modeller and dependent on the location where the fence is being used. Once the location of the fence and the approximate alignment have been determined, a small (1.5mm diameter) drill piece in a pin-vice can be used to bore holes in the scenery or baseboard at the points required for the fence posts. The depth of the hole should be approximately 3 to 4mm along the chosen alignment of the fence. If the holes for the posts are into the scenery, rather than into the baseboard, a small punch or small-diameter screwdriver can achieve the same result as a drill bit.

Each post in turn should be inserted into a hole and held in place with an appropriate adhesive. UHU-type impact adhesive works well, but it is also possible to use PVA wood glue or similar, if preferred. The fence posts can either be painted to the colour required before being cut from the sprue, or carefully painted once glued in place. It is down to personal preference and really depends on the

Fig. 253   Post and wire fencing from a OO-gauge Ratio kit provides a simple but realistic lineside feature.

Fig. 254   The posts are painted on the sprue before being installed on the layout; a hole for each post is bored using a 2mm drill bit held in a pin-vice.

Fig. 256   With the posts set, the plastic wires are fixed to the posts with liquid polystyrene cement, starting at the bottom; an extra pair of hands or wooden clothes pegs will be needed to hold the wire in place until the glue has set.

Fig. 255   Each post is fixed into its hole using impact adhesive.

Fig. 257 The completed fence, seen from the viewing side of the layout, forms part of a detailed scene and greatly enhance the overall impression.

accessibility of the posts once they have been stuck on the layout.

It is important to note that the posts should be set firmly in the holes before attempting to add the wires. The Ratio kit requires each wire to be glued into a notch in the fence post, so all the fence posts must be installed the right way round, so that the notch is on the same side all along. As supplied, the kit includes a roll of plastic wire, which can be quite springy when fixing to the posts, and does need a bit of pressure to be applied. A couple of wooden pegs from the clothes line will be invaluable to help hold the wire in place during the fixing process.

From my experience with this type of kit, you will achieve better results by working from the bottom

of the post upwards when applying the wires. Fix the plastic wire to the posts with spots of liquid polystyrene cement, a couple of posts at a time, allowing the glue to dry before moving on down the line. This is especially important where you want to bend the wires vertically along a fence line to follow the profile of the scenery, or at a lateral change of direction in the fence line.

The main tip here is: be patient! Allow the adhesive to set holding the wire to a couple of posts first, before trying to bend the wire for the change of direction to the next post. If necessary, you might want to consider pre-bending or shaping the length of wire to match the profile of the fence line, before attaching it to the fence posts. Working slowly and carefully in this manner, you should eventually be rewarded with a very convincing model fence on your layout.

An alternative approach to gluing the wires to the fence posts is to consider pre-drilling the fence posts using a small-diameter drill bit. The size of the drill bit is governed by the size of the wire being used, but on the fence posts provided in the kit a maximum size of, say, 0.5mm diameter, should be considered to reduce the risk of the fence posts breaking. Once the posts have been drilled, and then set in place, the wire can be threaded through the holes.

Great care is required when pre-drilling the posts, as the posts are thin and can easily break. Pre-drilling them while they are still attached to the sprues might help reduce the risk. As with the notched posts, though, it is important to make sure that the drilled posts are correctly fixed into the scenery, to ensure that the pre-drilled holes for the wires are parallel to the alignment of the fence, so that you can thread the wires through later.

One further variation on the construction of this type of fence kit would be the use of fine brass wire or fuse wire, instead of plastic, especially if you are planning to pre-drill the posts and thread the wire through. At this stage, you could almost dispense with the kit and scratch-build this type fence entirely, using suitably sized plastic rod section, pre-drilled for the posts, and a roll of fine fuse wire or brass wire. For a specific prototype location, scratch-building may be the preferred option, but for most cases the kit as supplied could be used as a generic type and the modeller could choose to focus their activity on rolling stock and larger, more visible structures on the layout. It is all down to personal preference, priorities and the time available to the modeller.

To be absolutely prototypically correct for this type of fence, the modeller should also consider adding the spacing bars between posts – these are not provided with the OO-gauge kit. In N-gauge this is probably not practical or good for your sanity, but in OO-gauge or larger scales, suitable spacer bars could be formed from scraps of fine plastic microstrip, appropriately painted and cut to length and then stuck to the wires. However, you may well take

the view that life is short enough and this fiddly task, while no doubt enhancing the overall model, is a step too far for a detail that few viewers of the layout are likely to notice. On my layout, I opted to omit it this time.

POST AND RAIL

One variation on the post and wire fence is post and rail, most often of timber construction. As with the post and wire fences, kits for the post and rail type of fence are readily available in OO-gauge and N-gauge from a number of suppliers, including Ratio and Wills. The N-gauge example produced by Ratio Models is available as either white (Ratio ref: 216) or brown (Ratio ref: 217) and the fence is supplied as four strips per pack on sprues, with each fence section being about 105mm in length.

For comparison, the OO-gauge kit from the same supplier is also available in two colours, white (Ratio ref: 424) and black (Ratio ref: 425), and each kit provides a similar number of fence sections, each approximately 210mm in length. In both scales, the fences are available in a couple of different base

Fig. 258 OO-gauge examples of plastic wooden fence kits for lineside and station platform locations.

Fig. 259   Use of wooden post and rail fencing as a boundary between the tram depot and highway in a corner of Tim Pollard's OO-gauge layout.

Fig. 260   Wooden fencing used as field boundaries for equine grazing on another part of Tim Pollard's 'Newcastle'.

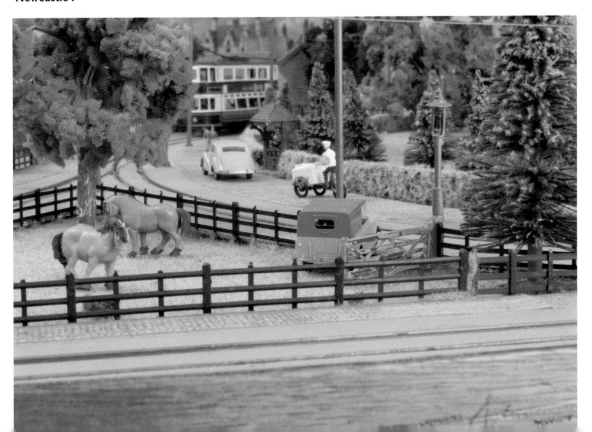

colours, which could be used straight from the pack without painting if desired. However, the fences will look more natural if they are painted to dull down the sheen of the plastic.

I used the N-gauge kit on my layout as both railway lineside fencing and roadside boundary fencing. First, the fence sections were painted while they were still fixed to the sprue, to make the job easier. The choice of fence colour is down to the modeller – a matt dark brown will give the impression of well-seasoned and stained timber fencing. Weathering could also be added to the fence or the odd rail could be cut to represent damage – all prior to removing the section from the sprue.

When the painting was completed and dry, the sections of fence were removed from the sprues and fixed to the layout. To aid installation, each post on the fence section has a smaller section moulded at the bottom, to be inserted into a pre-formed hole in the scenery. To make the holes for the fence posts, place the fence section along the preferred align-ment, mark the location of each fence post with a pencil and then made a suitable hole with a small-diameter (0.5mm) drill bit held in a pin-vice. The

Fig. 261   N-gauge wooden post and rail fencing being trimmed ready for use on the layout.

fence section can then be trial-fitted to make sure of the alignment and then glued in place. Use a spot of impact adhesive on the bottom of each fence post before pushing carefully but quite firmly into the pre-formed holes.

Fig. 262   N-gauge fencing installed as a railway/highway boundary on my 'Duddeston Junction' layout; changes in fence direction are easy to achieve by trimming the fence at the posts and then rejoining with adhesive to the desired direction.

This type of fencing can be easily bent or shaped, both vertically and horizontally, to match the profile of the scenery on the layout. It can also be cut and modelled to show changes of direction. It is important to note that, when joining two sections of fence together or changing direction, the post at the end of one of the sections should be removed to avoid a double post. If the end posts are removed carefully and cut flush with the rails, these 'spare' posts can be used to represent additional bracing posts at corners, joints or on long straight sections, as per prototype practice.

When gluing the fence into position, you need to be patient and get the fence lined up correctly, especially when joining two sections together or making corner joints. Extra time and effort spent making these joints look correct and square will pay off in the end, resulting in a more realistic-looking model.

One alternative approach to the use of a post-and-rail fence kit is scratch-building. In N-gauge this is likely to be quite fiddly, but it may have to be considered if there is a particular style of fencing

that you wish to create for a specific modelled location. Working in larger scales such as OO-gauge and O-gauge, the task of scratch-building does become slightly easier and less straining on the eyes, although conversely any small errors may be more obvious in these larger structures.

One example of a scratch-built post and rail fence in a larger scale is the metal version created for my O-16.5 layout. One of the central features of this new project is a road over-bridge, which crosses the railway lines on a skew, partially crossing a point junction. Further complexity is added by the fact that it is built at a rising gradient from the front to the back of the layout. At the front edge of the layout, there is provision for access from the bridge via a set of steps to access the station platform, for which a metal post and rail fence was required.

The design of the bridge structure does not contain a right-angle, other than the vertical point where the side walls meet the baseboard. Because there are no right-angles in the structure, the set of steps had to be scratch-built from individual layers of

Fig. 263 Metal post and rail fencing for a set of steps that give access to the station from the road bridge, built for my new 0-16.5 narrow-gauge layout (currently under construction).

Fig. 264 Close-up detail of the fence posts – nails and rails formed from 0.9mm brass wire, all built in situ.

card for each step, to match the profile of the adjoining bridge structure and the location on the layout.

Once the steps were completed, they needed fencing and the plan was to create something that would replicate cast-iron post and rail. There were no kits available that could be readily used for this purpose, so I started flicking through old articles and chatting through ideas with colleagues at the local club. In a flash of inspiration, I remembered watching a colleague create a fence on the club O-gauge layout, using nails for posts and fuse wire wrapped around them for the rails.

Adapting this type of approach for my layout, I decided that the fence posts should be formed from large flat-head panel pins, which were oval shape in cross section, approximately 35mm long and 3mm wide at the head. Holes were pre-drilled in the steps at appropriate points for the posts, and the panel pins were fixed into them with impact adhesive and then left to set. Each nail was checked to ensure that it was vertical and perpendicular to the baseboard before the glue was set.

To form the horizontal rails, I decided to use pre-cut sections of wire so that the rails would be straight and not deformed from being on a roll, as would have been the case with fuse wire. Brass wire of 0.9mm diameter was cut to the correct length and then fixed to the posts with cyano acrylate adhesive (superglue). As with the post and wire fencing, it was easier to start at the bottom rail and work upwards to the top rail. To get the rails evenly spaced and the same separation on each post, the position of each rail from the base was measured and marked, and then each was carefully added, checking to ensure that all was square.

The same procedure could be carried out for an OO-gauge layout, using smaller-diameter pins and, say, 1mm and 0.4mm brass wire for the rails. It might also be possible to reproduce something similar in N-gauge, but this might not do much for your eyesight or your sanity!

CONCRETE PANEL FENCING

Concrete panel fencing began to be more commonly used in the early to mid-twentieth century, as the use of pre-cast concrete became more widespread. This material was used in particular by the Southern

Fig. 265 Concrete panel fencing typical of the 1950s era, as used for the boundary to the small scrapyard on my N-gauge layout

Railway as a way of creating a 'modern railway' for the future. The aim was also to provide a coherent style across its region, following the Grouping in 1923, an amalgamation of many smaller companies to form the Southern.

Plastic kits are available in both N-gauge and OO-gauge to recreate the concrete-panel-and-post fencing style. The following example was used on my N-gauge layout 'Duddeston Junction', which, although not based exactly on the Southern Railway, does reference a fictitious location somewhere in the south of England during the 1950s and early 1960s. This was precisely the era when the use of concrete as a construction material was becoming much more widespread.

The N-gauge Ratio kit is supplied as two moulded fence sections, with ready-formed panels and posts, together with a sprue of additional fence posts and a selection of gates for use with the fence if required. On this project, I used two kits to create

fence sections on the layout. One kit was used to create a fence around a scrapyard to the rear of a small garage, while the second provided two fence sections and posts to create a single fence line. The gates from the kits were then available for use in conjunction with scratch-built brick wall sections, for the rear gardens of a terrace of houses on the same layout (see Chapter 5).

The first stage was to prepare the plastic kit parts by giving them a coat of base colour in a matt pale grey, a sort of concrete colour that I happened to have in my box of enamel paints. The aim was to try and represent a fence that had been installed for some time, so that the concrete looked weathered. Once the base paint coat had dried, dry-brush techniques were used to add various colours, to represent the effects of weathering – rust streaks from metal fixings and dirt from the industrial setting and proximity to the road and railway – as well as vegetation.

Fig. 266
The fence
set into the
landscape, with
bushes and
scrub vegetation
from Woodland
Scenics being
used to blend
it in.

Fig. 267   A close-up of the fence panels shows how dry-brushing techniques have been used to represent vegetation, grime and weathering effects.

CREATING THE EFFECTS OF WEATHERING

I have used dry-brushing techniques many times for weathering structures, buildings, vehicles and rolling stock, as well as other items for my layouts. There is no pre-determined pattern for my application of colours, but I tend to start with a palette and squeeze small amounts of various acrylic paints on to it, including red, yellow, orange, white, shades of brown and black, and occasionally a couple of different shades of blue or purple. Using a couple of relatively fine (say, sizes 1 or 3) good-quality brushes, I apply the colours randomly to achieve the desired effect.

The best way to achieve good results is to apply a series of browns and black first over the base colour with the larger brush, then go back over with the finer brush, adding spots and streaks with the brighter colours as desired. The base colour enamel paint provides a good surface on which to experiment with water-based acrylic paints, which can be watered down or mixed together, to achieve effective results relatively quickly. Depending on where the layout is located, you might wish to add a protective coat of matt varnish after finishing the painting.

The base colour and weathering effects may also be applied using air-brushing, if preferred, starting with the base colour enamel and then adding the various shades to achieve the desired effect. You might still need to use a fine brush to add small details, depending on your ability with the air brush.

Fig. 268 A selection of the fine brushes and paints used for the work on the fencing; good-quality fine brushes are better value in the long term than cheap ones.

Once all the painting had been completed, the fence sections were left to dry thoroughly, and the dried colours were checked to ensure that the correct impression had been achieved. On my layout, the painted sections of the fence were used to represent the boundary between an industrial tramway and a garage/car repair business. In order to give an untidy, run-down atmosphere to the layout, the fence needed to be heavily weathered, with an unkempt appearance.

The completed fence sections were fixed into the final position on the layout baseboard using impact

Fig. 269 *Wider view of the garage site to show how the fencing, hedging and scrub vegetation were used to develop the impression of neglect.*

adhesive. The first section of the fence line followed a curve in the tramway track bed, so some strategically placed wooden blocks and tools were used to hold the fence in position until the glue had set. When the sections were set in position, the paint along the lower edge of the fence, where it had been fixed to the baseboard, was touched up with enamel and acrylic paints. Additional detail was added in the form of vegetation (such as Woodland Scenics bushes), to contribute further to the run-down look.

The second section of fence to the yard area behind the garage was fixed in a similar way, although

Fig. 270 *Aerial view showing concrete walling used as lineside fencing, extending past the garage and along the approach lane to the site.*

here the fence could be attached to parts of the scenery and was partially self-supporting to form the yard area. Additional support was provided to the fence around the yard by two of the vehicles destined for the 'scrapyard' behind the garage building. The two model vehicles – an old Morris van painted green and the Morris Minor painted pale blue – were made up from white-metal kits. Once they had been painted and weathered, they were glued to both the baseboard and the fence to act as 'buttresses'. When the glue had dried, the paint was touched up, and scrub vegetation (Woodland Scenics products) was added, to bury the fence in to the landscape.

CORRUGATED METAL FENCE

On my OO-gauge layout I wanted to provide a section of corrugated fencing at the rear of the coal yard, at its boundary with the railway. It was to be based on fences that I had seen as a child on industrial sites next to the railway lines around Shrewsbury, where I grew up. There are several sources of appropriate

Fig. 271   Embossed plasticard sheeting can be used as fencing, roofing or to form buildings.

corrugated material that could be used to create a fence of this type, most notably in certain food and sweet boxes, which sometimes have a layer of heavy-gauge corrugated paper or thin card that is about

Fig. 272   OO-gauge corrugated plastic sheets were used to create a fence at the back of the station coal yard on 'Llanfair & Meifod'.

Fig. 273 Application of a suitable base colour to represent a rusting fence and a period sign are small details that help to develop the realism in the scene.

the right size in terms of the corrugations. Various model suppliers also produce ranges of plasticard with corrugated surfaces that can be used for buildings, roofs and fencing.

For my layout, I took an off-cut section of Wills corrugated plasticard sheet, which had been used to create the roof of a building. The off-cut piece was measured and cut to the right length and height for the proposed fence. The fence was then painted with enamel paints, using a rust brown as a base colour and then various colours and shades to create a weathered and run-down look.

The fence posts were formed from real wood, in this instance the matchsticks without the flammable heads that can be bought in large bags from most stationers and craft shops for modelling or craft purposes. Each post was cut to height then painted and fixed into pre-drilled holes in the baseboard with impact adhesive. When the posts had set hard, the painted fence panel was fixed to the posts and the baseboard, ensuring that the corrugated side of the plasticard was positioned correctly. In the real world, the upper sheet overlaps the lower sheet,

so that water running down the fence drains to the outside of the fence and not between the sheets, to the inside of the fence.

When the fence construction was completed and firmly fixed in place, additional details in the form of grass tufts and Woodland Scenics scrub were added, to blend the structure into the layout scenery. A couple of 'enamel' signs from Tiny Signs were then fixed to the fence to give some period atmosphere. All of this was achieved relatively quickly using a piece of material left over from a building project. Appropriate paint colours, bits of vegetation and lineside signage all contribute to the creation of a believable piece of scenery.

SECURITY FENCE

The use of security fences such as chain-link or palisade fencing is more appropriate for layouts based in the late steam and modern era, or certainly from the 1940s onwards. For example, the steel palisade fence seen in Fig. 247, alongside a railway line near Warrington, UK in 2016, was less common in the

Fig. 274 A security fence alongside the London Underground lines, behind the pre-fab housing, in a scene on Derek Lawrence's OO-gauge layout 'Gants Hill'. The fence was constructed from a Knightwing kit.

early part of the nineteenth century and before, so perhaps would not be appropriate for use on a layout of this period. Maybe there is a prototype somewhere that will prove me wrong!

A number of kits for this type of fencing are available in both N-gauge and OO-gauge from various suppliers, including Ancorton, Knightwing and Ratio. I have used some of the products from Ancorton on my N-gauge layout to create a security fence around a sewage treatment works and as a lineside fence to a section of the industrial tramway, where it runs alongside an access road.

The specific product represents a six-foot-high fence and is supplied as a roll of fine metal mesh for the fencing and laser-cut wooden fret for the fence posts. The etched metal film has see-through mesh at N-gauge and provides an extremely realistic representation of the prototype material, with excellent detail. The fence posts were painted before being removed from the fret, using a dull matt grey enamel paint to represent pre-cast concrete. The paint does not take easily to the wooden fret and can be streaky in appearance, but this all adds to the desired run-

down weathered effect, so I was happy to leave it after the first coat.

The instructions for the installation of the fence should be read carefully before starting. The roll

Fig. 275 There are a number of plastic fence products available for the modeller.

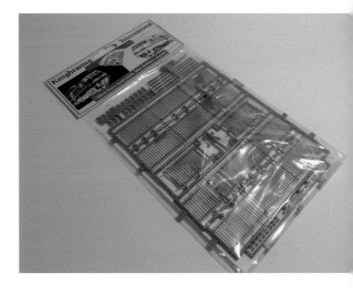

Fig. 276 The wire-mesh fencing in N-gauge, from the Ancorton range of specialist products, is actually see-through.

Fig. 277 It is advisable to instal the laser-cut wooden posts from the fret before adding the wire mesh; the finished fence adds a new level of detail to a layout.

of wire mesh used for the fence is supplied rolled and is taped to prevent it springing open. As soon the tape is cut, it will spring open to its full length – the metal has sharp edges, so take care when handling it.

Before removing any of the posts from the fret, check it carefully – not all of the laser-cut wooden posts are the same length. The fret not only supplies the standard fence posts, but also a number of shorter posts with angled ends, which are intended

Fig. 278 Use of the wire-mesh fence at the sewage treatment plant in the corner of the layout helped create an accurate representation of such sites, which are seen at many locations around the country.

for use as the diagonal support posts on long straight sections or at corners. These angled posts are fiddly to add and as per the instructions should be fixed to the vertical posts before the mesh fence has been fixed to the main upright posts. As long as you take note of the advice given in the instructions, and do not rush the installation of the fence, the end result will be a very convincing model of the prototype.

The instructions recommend that the fence posts, once painted, should be glued in to pre-drilled holes in the baseboard, with the holes located at approximate 20mm centres along the alignment of the fence. Installing this type of fence is a bit like constructing a fence in the real world. The posts need to be installed first and then the fence added.

The installation will be made easier if you decide on the alignment of the fence first, marking the route on the baseboard with a light pencil line and the location of each post at approximate 20mm centres. With a 0.5mm-diameter fine drill bit held in an Archimedes drill, make holes 3 to 4mm deep at each post location, then dip the end of each post in PVA glue and insert the posts into the holes. Leave the posts for 24 hours for the glue to set, then add the angled

posts as required at corners and at regular intervals on straight sections.

It might be wise to check that the posts are as near vertical as possible before the glue sets, although the odd post at an angle does not matter, as this is likely to reflect the real thing better. Posts often move due to soil creep on slopes and of course some may have been set not quite straight when first installed.

When all of the fence posts have set firm, cut the metal mesh to the correct length for each straight section of fence, ensuring that the joints are at corners or changes of direction of the fence. The mesh can be cut with a pair of good-quality sharp scissors or brass fret cutters if you have them. The mesh is then fixed to the fence posts by applying spots of impact adhesive to the sides of the posts and then pressing the mesh against the posts. Use small wooden blocks to keep the mesh in place against the posts until the glue has hardened off.

For the fence around the sewage treatment works it was relatively easy to cut the mesh into three straight sections, with the joints at the corner posts. However, where I used the mesh fence alongside the access road and tramway, installing the mesh was a little more difficult as I completed the whole length as one section, carefully curving the mesh to match the radius of the track before fixing. While the glue set, I used clothes pegs to hold the mesh in place against the posts at one end of the fence, and wooden blocks to keep the mesh in contact with the remainder of the posts.

It was fairly easy to bend the mesh fence to follow the curve of the road and track bed and this also helped with holding the mesh in place. Once I was happy with the position of the fence I left it for 24 hours to ensure the adhesive had hardened off, before removing the blocks and the peg. I opted to leave the mesh fence unpainted, but it should be possible to add colour, as long as you take care not to obscure the fine mesh detail by applying too heavy a coat of paint. The best results would probably be achieved using an air brush.

Another common type of security fence seen around these days on industrial sites, secure sites such as prisons and other sites where access is prohibited, is the metal palisade fencing formed from galvanized or painted metal rails held vertically, often with pointed tops to the rails and sometimes seen

with strands or rolls of barbed wire on top. This type of fence would be good to model for a modern-era model railway layout, with some form of industrial land use or secure site.

In OO-gauge, Knightwing produces a kit (ref: PM121) of a palisade-type security fence that is often found around factories and other industrial settings. The kit is produced in a dull grey plastic and could be used straight from the pack if required. However, a coat of paint to give it a more matt finish would enhance its appearance. The fence is supplied with 'feet' for the fence posts or it can be fixed direct to the baseboard – the choice is up to the modeller and the location intended for the fence.

The kit does not include any barbed wire, but this can be represented by using one of the kits supplied by Ancorton and others, or scratch-built using cotton thread soaked in PVA glue and then either used as strands of wire, or rolled to represent coiled wire. To use barbed wire either coiled or as strands, the fence posts will need to be increased in length. Prototype examples of this type of fence indicate that these post extensions should be angled out from the fence line, to discourage climbers. Plasticard micro-

Fig. 279 The fence panels of the OO-gauge security fencing can be used straight from the pack, but the effect will be improved by dulling down the plastic sheen with matt paints.

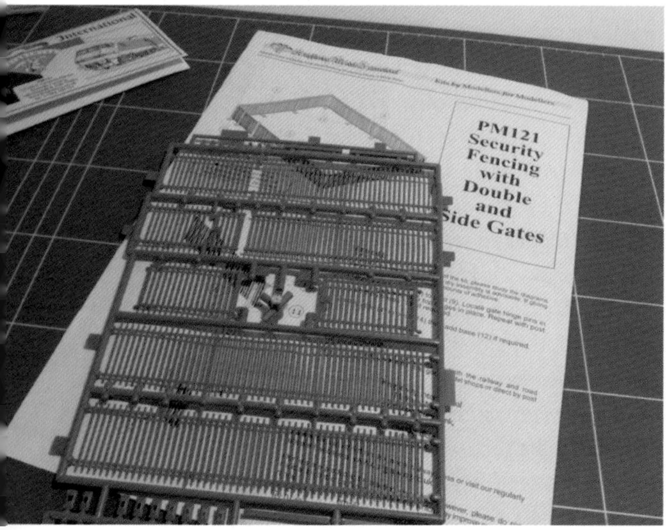

Fig. 280 A variety of fixings are included in the kit to enable the modeller to customize it to suit a particular layout location.

strip of the right size can be easily cut and glued to the plastic fence posts to recreate this modified fence if required. Once it has been painted, it should provide a realistic-looking fence.

The Knightwing kit includes sufficient fence sections and gates to create a compound approximately 130mm by 180mm, with a set of double gates. The height of the fence is about 28mm, depending on whether the feet are used. The configuration of the fence is flexible to meet the modeller's requirements and includes gate posts and hinges, and a separate pedestrian gate, as well as additional palisade posts to join sections of fence together. Using more than one kit will allow the modeller to create an impressive fence for an industrial or secure site.

The gate sections are wide enough that they can be used to provide a representation of either a road access or private railway siding access point to the site being modelled, opening up a wide variety of potential uses for the kit. As supplied, the gates can be modelled open or closed as they are not hinged.

Adapting the kit to provide opening gates is certainly not beyond the realms of possibility.

A relatively new development in OO-gauge security fencing for modern-era layouts is the recently released (2016) kit from Wills, which represents steel palisade fencing. The fencing is available in two kits; one includes a selection of fencing panels and gates (Wills ref: SSM316) and the second just fencing panels (Wills ref: SSM317). To model the modern era, that is, post-1980, the use of these kits is essential as lineside fencing in urban areas, as well as for industrial sites. The kits benefit from the latest plastic-moulding techniques, and the level of detail is such that the individual palisade strips of fence even include the spike detail at the top of each bar.

CATTLE PENS

My OO-gauge layout 'Llanfair & Meifod', based on a rural mid-Wales branch-line location, has a cattle dock that was based on the popular Ratio kit, which

Fig. 281   A common sight on steam-age railways was the cattle dock, recreated here in OO-gauge from the Ratio kit.

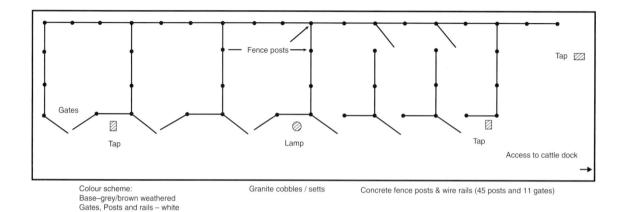

Colour scheme:
Base–grey/brown weathered
Gates, Posts and rails – white
Ironwork – black

Granite cobbles / setts

Concrete fence posts & wire rails (45 posts and 11 gates)

Fig. 282 Sketch plan drawn up to extend the cattle and sheep holding pens at Llanfair Station on my OO-gauge layout.

makes up into an excellent model. To extend the livestock holding facilities further, I recreated part of what would have been the wider livestock pens and cattle, typical of the market-town location. The concrete posts and wooden pen gates for the live-stock pens were created from the Ratio kit (Ratio ref: 419), which is of the same style as the cattle dock kit (Ratio ref: 502).

Using the parts in the kit I planned out on paper an area of pens and, from this, the number and location of posts and gates. These were then duly painted in the same colour scheme as used on the cattle dock. A base for the pens was created first using sheets of Ratio granite sets plasticard to represent cob-blestones, painted a base colour of grey-brown and then weathered.

Fig. 283 Landside view of the pens, with the station staff member opening the gates for new arrivals.

Fig. 284 Railside view of the pens; note the use of scenic materials to blend the structure in to the landscape.

The sketched layout of the livestock pens was overlain on the base sheets and the locations for the posts were marked. Holes were then drilled into the plasticard and the posts were fixed into the holes using liquid polystyrene adhesive. Once the posts were set, the metal railings were added to form the pens using 0.45mm-diameter brass wire threaded through the pre-drilled holes in the fence posts. Installation of the wire railings is best done by starting at the bottom rail and working upwards. A dab of impact adhesive was added at each end of the inserted wire to hold it in place. When dried, the posts and adhesive were touched up with paint to hide the glue.

Fig. 285 Sheep prepared for the pens in groups based on pen sizes.

Fig. 286 To make placement and removal of the livestock quicker and easier during an exhibition, they were glued to a slice of clear plasticard sheet, which may be placed or removed easily with a pair of tweezers.

The gates were then added to the pens and the paintwork touched up as required. Further detail was added around the pens, including vegetation and trackside signage. A member of the station staff was made from a slightly modified Dart Castings level-crossing keeper; he is still closing a gate, but on a cattle pen rather than at a level crossing!

The finishing touch was the addition of livestock. My idea was for the livestock not to be permanently stuck in the pens, either here or on the adjacent cattle dock, but to be removable, to create variety on the rolling stock movements on the layout. In the real world, for most of the time the pens would have been empty, only being used at the weekly cattle markets. To achieve this, I cut some clear plasticard into appropriately sized areas to match the size of each pen and then fixed sheep, pigs or cattle as required to each of the plastic bases. Each group of livestock on its plastic base can be lifted in or out as required with a pair of tweezers, so that the pens are not permanently occupied. The use of the clear plasticard means that the underlying base of the pens is not obscured, as it is almost invisible from a normal viewing distance.

STATION FENCING

The subject of station fencing could form a whole chapter, if not a substantial part of a book in its own right, with each individual railway company having its own preferences in terms of material types and styles. Indeed, some of the fence types already covered here would have been the style of station fencing for some railway companies. There follows therefore some general guidance on types of fence rather than a detailed description of the myriad diversity of fence styles and materials by railway company.

The careful selection and use of station fencing on a model railway plays an important part in creating a realistic representation. The fence styles and materials used are a good indicator of the railway company, era or region that you are trying to create in miniature. Reference to old photographs of stations, reproduced in books such as those by Paul

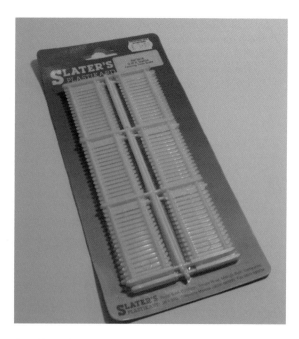

Fig. 287   O-gauge station fencing of the wooden post and rail type, typical of the GWR.

Karau (1977 and 1978) and many others, will aid in identifying the different types of station fencing that you might wish to recreate on your layout.

The station pictured in Fig. 246 shows a range of fence styles, including GWR wooden station fencing and metal spear fencing, as well as more recent wire chain-link fencing. Fig. 258 includes a selection of fencing kits available in OO-gauge, including station fencing, while Fig. 287 shows a similar type of fence but in O-gauge, showing the greater level of detail that is possible at this scale. Fig. 288 also shows typical Great Western Railway wooden station fencing. Station yard areas might typically use post and wire or timber post and rail fencing.

Installation of the platform fencing on my 'Llanfair & Meifod' layout was carried out once the platforms had been constructed in situ on the station board of the layout. In this instance, the platform edging was formed using the standard Peco product (LK-61 and LK-67), but, instead of using the adhesive pre-coloured stone sheeting, Wills sheets of dressed-stone walling (Wills ref: SSMP202) were cut to size and glued below the upper profiled edge.

Fig. 288   OO-gauge station fencing installed at Llanfair Station on my layout.

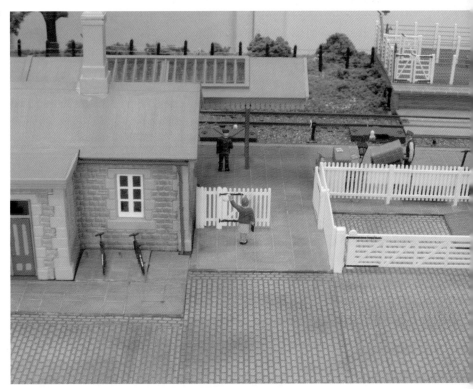

Fig. 289   The provision of fencing and gates around the building and access to the platform makes a nice finishing touch to the station.

The edge sections were then fixed to the baseboard and the space between the edging strips packed with polystyrene sheet. The top surface of the platform was formed using more Wills embossed sheets of paving stones (Wills ref: SSMP221), suitably painted and weathered.

The platform fencing used on this layout was the Ratio GWR wooden fencing style (Ratio ref: 420 and 421), available in moulded white plastic. I opted to paint the fence using a matt white enamel paint, to reduce the sheen. When ready, the fence, gate and ramp sections were laid along the platform and arranged to work out the sequence required. With the arrangement decided, the location of each fence post was marked on the platform surface using a pencil and then a hole was drilled with a 2mm-diameter bit, to a depth of about 3 to 4 mm. The depth required for the holes was measured on the sections of fence so that the bottom of the fencing was not touching the platform surface. The fence was then fixed in position with impact adhesive, starting at the station building end and working along the platform. When the fence was set in position, station name boards, platform seating, passenger and staff figures, as well as other equipment and buildings, were all added.

SCENERY FENCING

There are a number of other fence types and uses that should be considered by the modeller when building the scenery away from the railway land on a layout. These can be made either from specifically designed kits or scratch-built to suit the location.

HIGHWAY FENCES AND SAFETY BARRIERS

As with railways, highway land is often demarcated by a fence, wall or hedging, or most often a combination of these boundary types. If you want your layout to represent the real world accurately, it is important that, where you have modelled highways, you include some form of boundary marker. If you are modelling a real location, then observations of the roads in the area, either by visiting the site or by referring to photographs of the relevant era, should provide you with information as to what type of boundary to use.

Many of the fence types described earlier are likely to be equally applicable for use as highway boundaries as for railways. This means it is possible to adapt the kits for railway fencing to suite a modelled highway layout. By way of an example, on my N-gauge layout I used the Ratio post and rail fencing as a boundary for the roads on part of the layout, as well as field boundaries, combined with various Woodland Scenics products to represent hedging (see Fig. 262).

Another important aspect of modelling fences on highways is that in certain locations there will be safety barriers to prevent vehicles leaving the road inadvertently, for example, at corners or where a road passes alongside a steep valley. Modelling these types of details will help create the impression of a model of the real world.

These types of barriers can be scratch-built or made from modified kits. For my N-gauge layout, I used fence sections from the Ratio trestle bridge, mounted on a low wall to represent this type of highway barrier. Another section of the same fence was also utilized to represent a safety barrier around the fuel tanks in the goods yard.

WOOD PANEL FENCING

A relatively new development in model railways in both OO- and N-gauge is the use of laser-etched wood for structures, including fences. One example of this type of very useful product is the wood panel fencing from the Gaugemaster range, which can be used for gardens.

In the OO-gauge examples shown here, the products represent standard six-foot-high larch-lap type fencing and a similar larch-lap type of fence, with a decorative lattice trellis along the top of each fence section. Each kit contains three fence and post sections of approximately 100mm in length, giving a total fence length of about 300mm.

Careful examination of the fence sections shows that each length includes the fence posts, with the post omitted at one end to allow sections to be joined together without the need to remove

Fig. 290 *Highway barrier fencing for my N-gauge layout, recycled from a bridge kit and mounted on top of the brick retaining walls.*

Fig. 291 *Another use of the same fencing type, this time as a safety barrier around the tanks at the fuel depot.*

posts. When fixing these fence types to a layout, it is important to make sure you have the sections joined together the right way round. These products can be left as natural wood as supplied, or painted as required, before fixing to your layout with UHU-type adhesive.

SLATE FENCES

Specific to parts of North Wales in particular is the use of sheets of slate standing on end to form a fence, often with wire intertwined to hold the sheets together. This type of fence is very region-specific but for a layout based on a North Wales prototype,

Fig. 292   A selection of laser-cut wooden fences and plastic kits for garden boundary fencing in OO-gauge to enhance the scenery on a layout.

it provides a unique fencing style and something that should give a layout the feel of being set in the correct area. As far as I know, there is no kit available to reproduce this type of fence in model form.

However, the 'sheets' of slate can be reproduced by cutting appropriately sized pieces of black plasticard and then gluing them with impact adhesive along the fence alignment. A dark-coloured thread can be used to represent the wire.

SNOW FENCES

The snow fence is a type that is perhaps less common in the UK, but examples can be seen alongside roads in the upland parts of the country. As the name suggests, it is designed to reduce the risk of snow drifting across roads or railway lines, and thus blocking important lines of communication and trade. In model form, it could be represented with a picket-fence-type structure, formed from one of the fence kits that are available, or scratch-built.

WILDLIFE FENCING

As part of more recent road and railway projects, there is a requirement to complete an Environmental Impact Assessment, with the aim of informing the design process and identifying particular measures to reduce the impact on the environment. Many highway construction projects, and the HS1 link, have included the use of specially designed fences

Fig. 293   Scratch-built rough timber fencing to the yard of a garage scene on Tim Pollard's OO-gauge layout.

Fig. 294   Convincing landscaping and garden fencing, as well as many other small details in this O-gauge scene in a corner of Pete Waterman's 'Leamington Spa' layout.

to keep out wildlife or to direct wildlife away from the road or railway to specially constructed crossing points. These could be green bridges or tunnels, or underpasses.

In model form, this may not seem to be a priority that needs to be created on your layout. However, if you are modelling the modern era or maybe something such as HS1, it could be an interesting prototype detail addition.

CHAPTER SEVEN

DETAILING MODEL RAILWAY INFRASTRUCTURE

BRINGING A LAYOUT TO LIFE

There are a number of ways to bring a layout to life, with the addition of mini-scenes that allow the modeller to provide extra detail. The scenes described here are all based on my experience in constructing layouts in N-gauge, OO9 and OO-gauge, both at home and for my local model railway club.

All the skills and techniques that are used in the creation of tunnels, embankments, walls and fences can be applied, with certain adaptations, to other modelling tasks on a layout. The guidance here is all based on my experience, but it is important to recognize that the techniques described here are not the only way to achieve the results.

PLANTING A HEDGE

Adding a hedge to a layout makes an interesting alternative boundary marker, providing some variation from the more common walls and fences. Ready-made hedging is available from a number of suppliers and can be adapted or used straight from the packet.

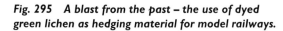

Fig. 295   A blast from the past – the use of dyed green lichen as hedging material for model railways.

Fig. 296   More modern scenic materials include the Woodland Scenics products that can be used for hedging and climbing vegetation.

I have used various methods over the years on different layouts. One material that has been around for many years, and is still available today, and is a common sight on many model railway layouts, is dyed green lichen to represent hedging, as well as bushes and scrub vegetation.

On my OO-gauge layout I used finely detailed hedging produced by the Dutch manufacturer Anita Decor and originally available through International Models in the UK. One of their products was a very realistic-looking hedge, available as both a field hedge and a more formal manicured garden hedge. Both products were reasonably priced and could be adapted in a variety of ways into the scenery vegetation on a layout. One variation on the field hedge also included small tree saplings, making this a very versatile product when modelling rural and suburban areas.

Fig. 297 A most convincing model field hedge in OO-gauge, produced by Anita Decor of the Netherlands, seen here in use on my OO-gauge layout.

Fig. 298 A very realistic product for a more formal garden hedge, utilized here on my OO9 micro-layout.

For the OO9 micro-layout 'Gylchfan', which I built some years ago, I used some of the finer garden hedging, cut in half heightwise, to provide a low hedge to a cottage vegetable garden adjacent to the narrow-gauge line.

I used an OO-gauge product from Gaugemaster (ref: GM160 or GM 161) on my new N-gauge layout as a high garden hedge between two rear gardens for a row of cottages. It was also used as the front garden boundary of a large detached house on the same layout (*see* Fig. 225).

These products for the various OO-, OO9- and N-gauge layouts were all fixed to the baseboard or scenery using PVA-type glue, with the hedging

Fig. 299 A flexible hedge product that is useful for OO-gauge layouts and can be flexed to suit the landscape.

held in place or pinned temporarily until the glue had set.

EMBANKMENT CULVERT AND WATER CHANNEL IN OO-GAUGE

On the OO-gauge 'Llanfair & Meifod' layout, I wanted to try and create a slow-moving stream or ditch waterway, with undergrowth and reeds, to enhance the open rural nature of this section. I built the railway line on an embankment using open-top baseboard construction, with a raised plywood track bed and expanded polystyrene blocks, to get the general land form. The base of the waterway or ditch was a piece of thin plywood set at the base of the embankment level. Off-cuts of timber were used to hold the base in place on the open baseboard frame.

Fig. 300 OO-gauge garden hedging in use on my N-gauge layout as a formal high hedge.

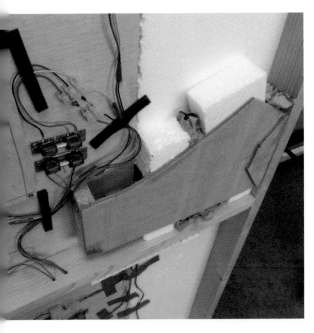

Fig. 301   Lowered section of the plywood baseboard for the drainage channel on my OO-gauge layout.

A culvert kit from Wills (ref: SS38) was used to provide a guide to the height of the embankment and the subsequent depth of the water channel or ditch below the rail level. With the timber former in place, the section below the railway embankment was painted matt black, to give the impression of a long culvert under the main line and adjacent yard area. The alignment of the channel was marked roughly with pencil and then the base of the channel was painted various shades of grey and brown, to represent shallow, slow-moving water. Green streaks were also added to represent vegetation in the water.

Once the colouring was satisfactory, the surface was coated liberally with satin varnish, allowing at least 24 hours between successive coats. Satin varnish gives a sheen like water, but is not as shiny as a gloss, which would be rather unrealistic for this location. With the 'water' completed, the surface land form was added, using my preferred technique of plaster-impregnated bandage strips laid and

Fig. 302   A water channel formed using paints and varnish for the slow-moving water; long grasses and bullrushes represent waterlogged ground.

Fig. 303   Representations of gorse bushes, created using Woodland Scenics large shrubs overlain with yellow flowering mesh held on with dabs of PVA glue.

shaped over the polystyrene forming block. Further undulations in the surface were provided by the use of small scrunched-up pieces of paper. When the plaster bandage had set hard, it was painted with normal emulsion paints, using various shades of green, brown and grey to provide the basic land-form colouring.

On top of the basic painted land form I used a selection of scenic materials from the Woodland Scenics range, to create the rough grass covering. Additional bushes and trees were added using the coarser foam materials, along with sea-foam tree pieces, suitably trimmed and cut to represent small trees and saplings. These were randomly planted on both banks of the channel.

Gorse bushes were formed using lumps of the coarse foam hedging/bush material from Woodland Scenics, suitably fixed to the landscape and then finished with bits of the fine mesh yellow flowering vine product draped and glued over the top. From a distance this looks quite realistic, especially when viewed as part of the overall scenic setting of the layout. Laser-cut reed plants from Noch (ref: 14102) were planted in to the edges of the water channel, along with individual flowering plant products from

suppliers such as Silflor and MiniNatur, for example, the small red-orange-coloured flowers (Silflor ref: 998-22).

The final addition to this scene was a fisherman and his basket, standing on the edge of the stream seeing what he can catch. The pieces came from Dart Castings (ref: MLVI) and were painted with a

Fig. 304   Wild flowers added to the banks of the channel using specialist flowering plant mesh produced by MiniNatur.

Fig. 305   The addition of a fisherman, with a cat's whisker fishing rod, completes a small detailed scene for the viewer.

mix of matt enamel and acrylic paints. The fishing rod was formed from a discarded whisker from our grey and brown striped tabby cat. (Obviously, I would not advocate plucking whiskers from a cat, but collecting and storing discarded ones for future use is perfectly reasonable – if a little mad, according to the rest of my family!)

A SEWAGE TREATMENT WORKS IN N-GAUGE

When I was trying to decide what to add in the corner of the upper level of 'Duddeston Junction', a small N-gauge layout with an urban/suburban theme, I had a flash of inspiration. Having worked many years ago for a couple of the water companies investigating sites for new and redeveloped sewage treatment works (STW), it occurred to me that this might be the ideal scenic feature to include on the

edge of the urban area. The layout did not have space to model an entire sewage treatment works, but I could model one or two key elements to suggest a bigger site extending off scene.

Having laid the track and worked out the extent of lineside vegetation, I was left with a small, roughly triangular area of baseboard on which to build a representation of the STW. I decided that the key structures would be one of the typical circular treatment beds, and maybe a raised manhole inlet works, a pump house and an ancillary building.

The circular treatment or filter bed was scratch-built from card. The base was formed by drawing a circle around a pot on thick card and then cutting this out with sharp scissors. The side walls of the structure were then formed from thin card strips cut to the correct height, approximately 6mm, and glued around the edge of the base disc with PVA. The card strips forming the edge walls were laminated with

Fig. 306   A small sewage treatment works filling a corner on the upper level of a small N-gauge layout helps with the impression of an urban scene.

several thicknesses of strip to ensure a sturdy structure. When the glue had set, the whole structure was painted in a pale grey to represent weathered concrete.

The rotating sprinkler arm and central support (non-operating) were formed from scraps of plastic and wire. It would probably be feasible to make a rotating structure and motorize it, but I decided against it on this occasion.

Once the painted structure was dry and the rotating arm firmly fixed into the filter bed, I needed to add something to represent the aggregate found in this type of filter bed. Looking in my box of scenic materials, I realized that the aggregate could be reasonably represented by using Woodland Scenics N-gauge fine grey ballast. The ballast was applied and built up in several layers across the bottom of the filter bed, using the same method of application and gluing as for normal track ballasting.

Once the filter bed had been positioned on the site of the proposed STW, I made up a raised manhole chamber using scraps of plasticard and a small off-cut of the wire-mesh fence for the surface grid.

It seemed reasonable for the main pump-house building to be an older structure, so I adapted a Ratio engine-shed kit and fitted a new scratch-built roof. The roof was formed using a thin card base and then strips of card pre-painted to the colour of the roof tiles, cut into 2–3mm wide strips and scored and partially cut to represent individual tiles. These were laid over each other, starting from the bottom edge of the roof and working up to the ridge. This technique is copied from the Scalescenes kits, which I had previously used on the row of cottages elsewhere on the same layout. With the pump-house building completed, I added a small LED light into the structure, as part of a wider use of lights in the buildings on the layout to add further interest.

Fig. 307 Water-treatment bed fabricated from card and scrap bits of plastic and wire for the water sprinkler.

Fig. 308 A Ratio engine-shed kit converted to a sewage treatment works pumping station, with scratch-built tiled roof and internal LED lighting.

The final structure was part of a pre-cast plaster item obtained from Ten Commandments, intended to represent a low-relief maintenance building. The cast was painted using acrylics to represent a typical 1950s industrial-type structure and glued right in the corner of the layout against the back scene.

The filter bed, buildings and ancillary structures, including a section of scratch-built low red-brick wall fixed to the back scene, meant to represent the edge of a sludge drying bed, were then arranged on the baseboard. Roadways and grass areas were marked and then the structures were fixed in place with suitable adhesive. Where the pump-house building was

to be located, a hole was drilled in the upper-level baseboard and the main baseboard, to feed the wire connection for the LED light to the power supply.

The roadways on such sites were typically concrete sectional roads, and this was represented by printing off additional concrete panel road sections from a Scalescenes garage kit (Scalescenes ref: T017) and rearranging them to fit the road plan drawn on the baseboard.

When the roadway had been glued in place, the grass areas were formed in the normal way using Woodland Scenics fine turf products. The final element was the addition of a couple of figures, suitably posed (Peco and Scenecraft), and then a boundary fence around the STW site. The fence was formed from an Ancorton mesh material (see Chapter 6). The overall result was effective when viewed from a distance and certainly provides something a bit different to add to the scenery of a layout.

AN OCCUPATION CROSSING AND WALLED LANE IN OO-GAUGE

After exhibiting the OO-gauge layout, 'Llanfair' (before it was extended to become 'Llanfair & Meifod'), for the first time at the Jersey Model Railway Club exhibition in 2009, I wanted to insert an additional scenic board between the station and the fiddle yard exit for the next exhibition. This would increase the running length on the scenic side of the layout, as well as demonstrating some changes and enhancements since the first showing.

I built a short straight section of scenic board and wanted to create a focal point to interest viewers. In the quest for something different, I came up with the idea of an occupation crossing, with the track towards the back of the baseboard and a raised scenic area at the front of the baseboard. This meant that the viewer had to look through the scenery to see the railway line rather than having scenery at the back of a layout.

To focus the viewer's eye on the crossing point I modelled a walled sunken lane through the scenery from the front of the layout to the crossing, drawing the eye to this feature. To one side of the lane there would be a wooded area and to the other an area of hillside grazing for sheep. The baseboard was built as an open-top construction, with the only solid board top along the area of the track bed at the back of it. The entire front section of the baseboard was then built up, using expanded polystyrene blocks fixed direct to the timber framing with impact adhesive.

Fig. 309   A local freight train including scratch-built rolling stock passing the occupation crossing on the branch line to Llanfair.

Fig. 310 Walled lane approach to the crossing from the public viewing side of the layout; the shepherd is watching his sheep as well as the passing freight train.

Once it had been fixed in place, the polystyrene was carved to achieve a basic outline for the scenery. Plaster bandage was then used to form the surface topography, using the same method as you would for forming embankments. The polystyrene provided a good base material for the sunken lane and rock outcrops. The lane was formed by carving down through the upper layers of the polystyrene to the right level, and then carving and shaping the material further to represent a rocky surface to the track.

When the required contours had been achieved, I painted the entire scenic area using normal emulsion paints of varying shades of green and grey. This was then enhanced by painting the track bed with matt enamel paints in varying shades of grey, to get the desired colour base. Rock outcrops were formed in a similar way, the texture of the carved and painted polystyrene being a reasonable representation of the type of rock I wanted to model. If I were tackling the process now, I would probably consider adding some cast rock outcrop pieces, using the moulds

Fig. 311 Crossing constructed from a Ratio kit and built up in situ with the fencing and stile; in the background, the local farmer leads his horse up the walled lane back to the farm (which is off scene).

Fig. 312   Train-spotters at the stile and sitting on the wall waiting for the next train.

Fig. 313   Use of ready-to-plant walls and polystyrene sheet for the landscape results in plenty of foreground scenic detail and creates the impression of a railway in the scenery passing to the rear of the baseboard.

that were used for the rock outcrops on the club's North American-themed layout (see Fig. 191).

The areas away from the lane were then marked for tree planting and the building of boundary walls. All of the trees on this section of the layout were made using Woodland Scenics tree armature kits, in varying sizes and shapes, from small trees to representatives of semi-mature standards. None of the trees are meant to be specific species; it was more to create an overall impression, with plenty of variation in the colouring of the trunks and the foliage material. Gorse bushes were formed using lumps of Woodland Scenics' coarse foam hedging/bush material, fixed to the landscape and draped with bits of the fine mesh yellow flowering vine product.

The clear ground areas were treated with a mix of Woodland Scenics turf products. The walls to

the lane and railway boundary were formed using the Skaledale ready-to-plant items, suitably colour-washed and weathered to a more realistic colour for the area being modelled. The walls were installed and fixed in place using the normal methods (see Chapter 5).

The hilly area to the side of the lane bounded by walls was then detailed to represent a hill farm sheep-grazing field. A small hut from the Wills Grotty Huts & Privy kit (ref: SS19) was modified for use as an animal shelter. Sheep were added to the field, along with a shepherd and his trusty dog. The wall sections contained a style to connect fields together for live-stock and people to use. I chose to model this with a fence section barrier to prevent sheep movement out of the grazing area, based on practice observed on hill farms in the real world. The area next to

Fig. 314 An air of neglect has been created with a derelict industrial landscape that includes an abandoned and partially lifted triangular junction and a disused boarded-up signal box.

the grazing field was modelled as rough ground, with trees, scrub vegetation and falling-down wall sections adding to a sense of abandonment.

The occupation crossing was the Ratio kit (ref: 509), unmodified and modelled in the closed to non-railway track position. I included the styles for pedestrian access and sections of the standard wire and post lineside fence (see Chapter 6). I added scrub vegetation around the crossing as well as modelling the short section of lane between the railway and the edge of the baseboard. To complete the scene, I painted and added some train-spotters sitting on the wall and standing by the fence, as well as a farm worker leading a heavy work horse up the lane back to the farm.

All of the figures, including the horse, came from the Dart Castings range, while the sheep were from the Peco Modelscene range. At the last count there are more than 150 sheep fixed on the 'Llanfair & Meifod' layout, either in lineside scenes or waiting in the cattle dock to be taken to market.

AN ABANDONED JUNCTION AND SIDING IN N-GAUGE

I was having difficulty in deciding on an original idea for scenic modelling that might be that bit different

to fill a space at the front of my new N-gauge layout. The layout had an area across the front on the lower level that was too small for a large-scale industrial scene, but I wanted the use to be non-rural. After flicking through a few books, I hit upon the idea that eventually led to the name of the layout: to create an abandoned and partially lifted junction with an adjacent disused siding. All of this would help with the impression of an urban industrial railway system in decline.

While sketching out the plan for the lower level of the layout, the junction was notionally sketched in, with the siding parallel to the running line extending into the cutting. The idea was that this would have been a single through line with a junction in both directions possibly feeding an industrial site off scene. The name of the junction, 'Duddeston Junction', was picked at random from an atlas of UK place names – the real Duddeston is an area in Birmingham and does in fact have a railway station, but the name is the only link between my layout and the real place.

Using the sketch of the layout for the lower-level loop, I marked out the position of where the track would have been located for both the junction and the siding. Using pieces of track recycled from an old layout being dismantled at my local club, I placed a couple of sections of track to represent

Fig. 315 *The siding associated with the junction has been truncated from the running line and is beginning to be reclaimed by the vegetation.*

Fig. 316 *The points to the siding have been lifted and an old wagon is marooned in the siding, with old sleepers and sections of rail discarded beside the running line.*

the truncated chords of the junction and a length for the siding. The assumption was that, following the lifting of the points for the junction and siding, some of the old track had been left in place pending future removal – when the track maintenance teams eventually got round to it.

The pieces of track around the junction were heavily weathered with a variety of enamel paints and then scenic ground-cover materials (various Woodland Scenics products) were applied to this area of the baseboard. Bushes, saplings and small

tress were made up from sea foam and Woodland Scenics tree armature kits and 'planted' across the junction area, with the intention of showing that the natural vegetation was slowly reclaiming possession of the area.

The disused siding was laid on a thin layer of ballast and then weathered, and scrub vegetation was added in a similar fashion to the track sections at the junction. In addition, I took a Peco five-plank open wagon kit (ref: KNR-40) and painted and weathered this before fixing it permanently to the siding with impact adhesive. The wagon was modelled with one of the side doors hanging open and small sections of disused rail left in and around it.

A ROAD OVER-BRIDGE EXIT TO A FIDDLE YARD IN OO-GAUGE

On the first version of the OO layout 'Llanfair', the end board had a short scenic section to disguise the entrance to the fiddle yard. Having thought about how this might be achieved, I decided to construct a road over-bridge immediately in front of the back-scene board.

The road over-bridge was constructed from scratch at the entrance to the fiddle yard using sheets of Wills dressed stone for the abutments and wing walls, and girders recycled from an old Airfix turntable kit for the bridge walls.

The bridge design is based on the bridge at the GWR Fairford Station, as shown in Paul Karau's book (1977). Using the photographs in the book as a guide, I prepared construction drawings by hand for the structure on the layout. I drew out to scale a basic pattern for the component parts of the structure

Fig. 318   Polystyrene sheet was used to form the basic shape of the scenery and the embankment on either side of the bridge.

Fig. 317   Construction of the scratch-built over-bridge was carried out shortly after the track had been ballasted and tested.

at 4mm/ft, to work out how many sheets of stone I would need and to minimize waste of materials.

The bridge was then 'built' in situ on the layout once all the stonework had been cut out, painted and weathered. Polystyrene sheet was used as backfill behind the abutments and wing walls to form the embankment. A bridge deck was then formed from thick card and support girders were added underneath the deck, sitting on 'bearings' on top of the abutment walls, just like the real thing! Capping stones to the wall pillars were individual cut-outs from Wills paving slab sheets left over from other projects, and the capping to the wing walls was formed from roof capping stones.

A steep-sloped embankment was formed with the polystyrene to create a cutting with rock outcrops. Plaster bandage was used over the polystyrene to get the final land form and this was then coated with green emulsion paint as a base colour. A selection of Woodland Scenics turf products was then applied to the embankment and loose rock material was added

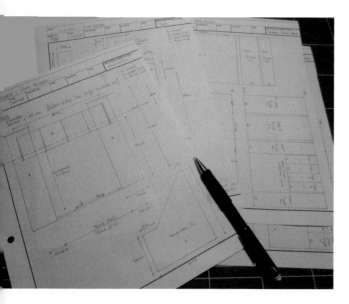

Fig. 319 Hand-drawn pattern sheets for the bridge were prepared to calculate the quantity of dressed-stone plasticard sheets required and the length of girder for the bridge deck.

Fig. 321 Off scene in the fiddle yard, hardboard was used for the back-scene board between the scenic section of the layout and the fiddle-yard area.

Fig. 320 Complete bridge and chapel scene framing the exit/entrance to the fiddle yard on 'Llanfair & Meifod'.

Fig. 322   The addition of a motorcyclist pausing to watch the trains and the Reverend leaving his chapel to walk to his car are small detail touches that bring a layout to life.

Fig. 323   Road signs and a textured road surface are further detail additions to the scene that make it more realistic.

using pieces of shredded cork, suitably painted. Scrub vegetation and grass tufts further enhanced the visual appearance of the scenery.

At the top of the embankment, I used Ratio post and wire lineside fencing as the boundary between the road and the railway cutting embankment. The fence line followed an 'S'-shaped route along the road edge. I found that fixing the plastic wire to the posts was a tedious task and could only be accomplished a couple of posts at a time. Failing to

allow the glue to set before moving on to the next post resulted in the wire coming away, as tension pulled the posts apart. With the benefit of hindsight, I would probably choose fuse wire instead of the plastic wire, which could be shaped to the length of the fence and hold its shape while fixing to the posts. Next time!

The road surface on the bridge and at the top of the embankment was formed from a thin layer of card, cut to the width of the road and glued to the upper surface of the polystyrene scenery blocks. This was painted a suitable grey colour to represent old asphalt. While the paint was still wet, fine sawdust was scattered on to the surface to give it a texture. When this had dried, a second coat of paint was applied to seal it all in. The result is a good representation of a weathered surface with some texture, which is often missing from roads on model railways.

A platelayer's hut and GWR Distant signal post were added at the lineside immediately before the road over-bridge; both are removable for transport of the layout, to guard against damage. The hut was set back into the embankment, necessitating a cut-out and leaving exposed 'rock face', all contributing to the scenic atmosphere that I was trying to recreate (see Fig. 320).

A LINESIDE GARAGE AND SCRAPYARD IN N-GAUGE

The basis of this mini-scene was the Scalescenes garage kit (ref: T017), downloaded and printed off from their website. According to the comprehen-sive instructions that come with the kit (which, as always, should be read fully before starting the build), the printed sheets need to be mounted on different grades of card. For this project, they were fixed to the card with PVA adhesive and then left to dry, weighted down under a couple of heavy books, to prevent the card curling.

The kit builds up in to a sturdy structure with both internal and external detail. It was supplied with a base representing concrete panels, which was fixed with PVA glue to the baseboard. Additional printed copies of the base were created and used to extend the representation of concrete pavement to part of the approach road to the site, as well as for the concrete sectional road at the sewage treatment site. The garage was glued in position on the base-board and additional details, including the external fuel pumps, vehicles and mechanics, were added to the scene.

To enhance the scene further, a ready-to-plant Nissen hut from the Graham Farish Scenecraft range (ref: 41-110) was glued in position adjacent to the access road. The hut was weathered with

Fig. 324 Scalescenes' N-gauge garage kit, downloaded from the website and built in card, forms a highly detailed focus for the garage scene, paired with the ready-to-plant Nissen hut from the Graham Farish range.

Fig. 325 Close-up of the scrapyard, showing the use of white-metal vehicles as props for the concrete panel fence, with partially disassembled Oxford Diecast period cars filling the yard.

acrylic paints and then creeper vegetation from the Woodland Scenics range was applied to add to the general air of industrial landscape.

Ratio concrete panel lineside fencing (ref: 219) (see Chapter 6) was used to form the scrapyard at the rear of the garage building. With the fencing complete, a number of cars were positioned in the yard, suitably weathered and distressed.

A WALLED COPSE AND OPEN MOORLAND IN OO-GAUGE

The new corner baseboard on the extended OO-gauge layout 'Llanfair & Meifod' was designed with an interchange station for the narrow-gauge and standard-gauge railway lines. The design of the new baseboard enables the standard-gauge line to turn through ninety degrees and as a result the scenery has been designed to bank up to the outside edge of the baseboard.

On the hill above the station, which also hides the return loop for the narrow-gauge track, I wanted to create a feature that would require the viewer to look around or through to get a view of the running lines. I decided that this area should represent more rural and isolated countryside and therefore I needed to identify a feature that would be typical of this type of surrounding.

Fig. 326 Wooded copse on my OO-gauge layout as viewed from the approach from the fiddle-yard end of the layout; there are gorse bushes in the foreground and the track curves away to the left through Meifod station halt on to Llanfair.

Fig. 327 Open moorland on the inside of the curve of the track disguises the tunnel entrance and separate fiddle yard for the narrow-gauge lines.

Fig. 328 At track-bed level the railway boundary is marked with a simple post and wire fence.

I quite liked the concept of a wooded hillside, but this would not have been modelled realistically within the available space. After a bit of research, I decided to create a small wooded copse and to define the boundary of this with a stone wall, for which I utilized more of the Skaledale wall sections that had been used elsewhere on the layout, but also including the section with a wooden field gate.

The area was marked out on the top of the raised scenic area and I set about preparing the ground

Fig. 329 At the opposite end of the wooded copse, a gate access is provided; in the foreground, laser-etched ferns and bracken by Noch are used to represent upland vegetation.

Fig. 330 Aerial view of the copse from the Meifod Station side, showing the wide variety of colour and texture on the trees.

Fig. 331 Low-level view showing that it is possible to see through the wood beneath the tree canopy – just like the real thing!

surface as a woodland floor before planting the trees. This included modelling undulations in the ground and then applying a blend of earth, soil and grass fine turf products from the Woodland Scenics range. The wall sections were painted and weath-ered (*see* Chapter 5) and then the boundary wall was positioned and fixed to the scenery. Additional ground cover and scrub vegetation products were applied after the wall was in place to hide the base of the wall and make sure there were no gaps.

With the walls in place and the ground covering set, it was time to plant the trees in the copse. I collected together a variety of deciduous tree types using pre-formed trees from the Scenecraft range and the sea-foam trees available as boxes from a number of suppliers. Although none of the model trees that I used represented specific species, the intention was to group them closely together in a random fashion to give the overall impression of a natural wood.

Working from one corner of the walled area, I started to plant the trees, trying to ensure that their canopies interlocked so that they were quite densely packed. By varying the height and colour of the trees, the overall effect was very pleasing. The added benefit was that the viewer could look through the gate and see under the tree canopy to view the woodland floor below.

To enhance the scene further, I used a variety of different-coloured flowering bushes from Silfur and MiniNatur and laser-cut ferns from Noch (ref: 14100). Homemade gorse bushes were added to the open ground around the walled copse and used on the top parts of the embankment sides to the railway cutting, to blend the mini-scene into the overall effect of the layout. The final touch was to add a bird-spotter (or train-spotter, depending on preference) standing at the top of the embankment, observing the scene through his binoculars.

A NARROW-GAUGE AND STANDARD-GAUGE INTERCHANGE IN OO-GAUGE

The premise behind the extension to the OO-gauge layout, to create 'Llanfair & Meifod', was the combination of narrow gauge and standard gauge on the same layout. The plan was to include a narrow-gauge feeder line to the standard-gauge branch line, to add

Fig. 332　Aerial view of Meifod interchange station with the standard-gauge track curving off to the right to the fiddle yard.

operational interest and to satisfy my interest in both gauges.

Inspired by the Ffestiniog Railway in North Wales and the Welshpool and Llanfair Caereinon line in mid-Wales, I looked for the best way of combining the two gauges in one layout. The opportunity came to build an interchange during the construction of an extension.

I opted to build the two new baseboards as open-frame structures and this enabled me to raise the standard-gauge line on a low embankment, while at the same time lowering the narrow-gauge line so that it could pass beneath the main line. Elsewhere on the new boards I constructed a goods interchange facility as well as shared cattle dock facilities for the narrow- and standard-gauge systems.

Fig. 333   Low-level view across the upland grazing areas to the standard-gauge line and the interchange sidings, with the narrow-gauge system beyond.

Fig. 334   Dual-gauge track (made by Tillig) and interchange facilities for goods and livestock are just some of the interesting details for the viewer.

The space left after the construction of the embankment structures allowed me to add a simple through station on both the narrow-gauge and standard-gauge lines. The narrow-gauge line is built between the bridge carrying the standard-gauge line over the narrow gauge and the tunnel taking the narrow-gauge line off scene to the fiddle yard. The station is built on a curve and includes a single siding for the storing of the occasional wagon. The platform was constructed from a single piece of 4mm plywood, cut to match the internal curvature of the track and then painted to represent an asphalt paving area.

The station building was formed from a Wills kit for a timber wayside station waiting room (ref: SS67). The basic kit as supplied was enhanced by some additional detailing, including the addition of a timetable board with GWR timetable, a notice board with a holiday poster for Jersey, an external modified gents' toilet kit (ref: SS65) and a platform seat. A passenger was added to the seat and a couple of station staff were also added to the scene, one of whom is washing the station windows. All the figures came from the Dart Castings range and were painted using a mix of enamel and acrylic paints.

The station sign is a notice board mounted on two sections of standard code 100 rail, as per typical prototype practice in remote rural areas. The station name was created on the PC and printed out and then mounted with PVA on the sign board. The sign states 'Meifod – Change here for Llanfair and trains to Welshpool and Shrewsbury'.

A (non-working) platform lamp from the Peco Modelscene range, suitably repainted in appropriate railway company colours, completes the narrow-gauge station scene. A flight of steps, a discontinued ready-to-plant item from the Hornby Skaledale range (ref: R8723), provides a link up to the standard-gauge station at the top of the embankment. From the top of the steps, a path leads up to the rear of the platform halt, where scratch-built steps formed from overlapping pieces of thick card lead up to platform level.

The standard-gauge station is meant to be a halt and was formed from two station halt kits produced by Wills (ref: SS25), together with a pagoda shelter kit by the same manufacturer (ref: SS35). The two timber platform kits were cut and modified to match the curvature of the line. This simply meant cutting the ends of each oblong section at an angle so that they could be joined up around the outside of the curve. Once they had been glued together with liquid polystyrene cement and then painted and suitably weathered, the structural adjustments to the kits were not noticeable.

Fig. 335 Steps connecting the narrow-gauge platform with the standard-gauge platform were partially built with modified ready-to-plant steps at the bottom and scratch-built card steps for the upper section.

Fig. 336   The narrow-gauge passes under the standard-gauge via the low girder bridge adapted from a Wills kit.

As the curve on the line is only a standard second radius at this point, due to limitations on baseboard size, there is a non-prototypical gap between the platform edge and the rolling stock. This was necessary to enable the outside cylinder locomotives and bogie stock to traverse the curves without catching the platform structure. However, from normal viewing distances, the discrepancy is not too obvious. This is because the scenery is designed to draw the eye away from it and on to other scenic details on this section of the layout, such as the walled copse on the hill above the station and the sheep grazing on the hills opposite.

The pagoda platform shelter is a typical GWR lineside feature; in this location, the structure kit (Wills kit ref: SS35) was modified with the addition of a window. This was based on a picture of a similar structure on a wayside station on the Bala Junction to Blaenau Ffestiniog branch, featured in one of the reference texts (Williams, 1976).

The halt station scene was completed with the addition of a non-working lamp from the Ratio range and a platform seat with a solitary seated passenger waiting for the train to stop. The station name board on the standard gauge is of the type that fixes to the platform fencing.

The over-bridge carrying the standard-gauge line over the narrow-gauge line was formed using the Wills occupation bridge kit (ref: SS28) as the basis, with some modification to the abutment walls, to ensure sufficient clearance for the narrow-gauge track passing underneath. I added the abutment walls and wing walls for the bridge at the same time as building the embankment, to ensure that the height of the track bed for the standard gauge was correct and flowed evenly across the bridge structure without any sudden steps.

The bridge walls were painted and weathered before fixing to the baseboard. A base colour of matt enamel was applied to the embossed plasticard, to give the general stone colour required, and then the parts were weathered by a combination of thin colour washes of a dirty off-white colour, enhanced with dry-brushing techniques using a mix of enamel and acrylic paints to achieve the desired finish. The track bed for the bridge was formed from the same plywood as used on the embankment and the bridge sides were suitably painted and weathered, and fixed to the side of the plywood section and the top of the abutment walls using impact adhesive.

The track for the narrow-gauge section was laid before the bridge was constructed, to aid with the painting and ballasting of the track. Once the abutments had been fixed in position, the ballast at the edge of the track bed was extended to the base of the walls. The standard-gauge track over the bridge was glued and ballasted in the normal way – for this section I opted to use a piece of set track for additional rigidity, as the track is curved at the location of the bridge and station. The track was painted and weathered before being fixed in position on the track bed.

A COTTAGE GARDEN ON AN OO9 MICRO-LAYOUT

The OO9 micro-layout 'Gylchfan' was intended as a test bed for a number of new scenic ideas that I wanted to try. At the front left-hand side of the layout, I decided to include a small cottage and vegetable garden as a detailed scene. I scratch-built a sandstone cottage, utilising Wills dressed-stone sheets (ref: SSMP202) painted a reddish-brown colour to

Fig. 337 A small scene created on the corner of 'Gylchfan': a small cottage with vegetable garden, largely scratch-built with a modified Ratio Station Porter Fig. for the gardener.

Fig. 338 The vegetables for the cottage garden on 'Gylchfan', with leaves created from tissue paper, pre-painted in varying shades of green and punched out using a variety of leaf-shaped punches.

Fig. 339 The paper leaves are glued one inside the other, and the leaves are folded up to create a plant-like feature.

Fig. 340 Air-dry clay is rolled into shapes for the various vegetables, such as marrows and cauliflower, painted in appropriate colours and then glued into the leaf clusters to form the plants. The plants are then glued in rows on to the prepared soil of the garden.

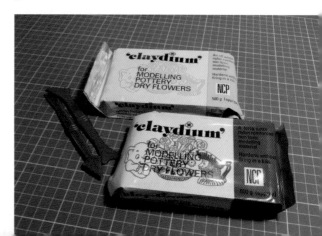

simulate the Old Red Sandstone that is typical of the area where the model was to be notionally set. The building also made use of one of the sets of windows and doors for scratch-builders from the same supplier (Wills ref: SS42).

The vegetable garden was made from carefully rolled and shaped pieces of air-dry clay, which was painted accordingly. The leaves of the potato, cabbage and cauliflower plants were made from painted green paper in different shades, inspired by an article in the March 2011 edition of *Railway Modeller*. The gardener figure was a suitably painted former railway porter, an old Ratio white-metal figure from my spares box.

A SIGNALMAN'S ALLOTMENT IN OO-GAUGE

One mini-scene on the approach to the main station on my layout 'Llanfair & Meifod' comprises the main station signal box with its attendant allotment. The signal box was constructed from the standard Ratio kit (ref: 503), and the small allotment and outside privy were added to make the scene more interesting. The privy came from the Wills Grotty Huts & Privy kit, whilst the elements of the allotment came from various sources.

The turned earth and vegetable rows, the compost heap and cold frame are white-metal products from a vegetable plot kit produced by Knightwing (ref: B70). These items were suitably painted with enamel base colours and weathered with acrylic paints. The rhubarb plants, another product from the Noch minis range of laser-cut plants (ref: 14108), completed the vegetation.

Fig. 341 An alternative method of producing a vegetable plot: white-metal castings from the Knightwing range, including a compost heap and cold frame, suitably painted and fixed to the layout next to the signal box.

Fig. 342 Rhubarb plants folded up from an etched fret (Noch), used to enhance the white-metal castings of the signalman's allotment.

RESOURCES

BOOKS AND ARTICLES

The following books and articles have been used as reference material in the preparation of this book:

Andress, M. 1981 *PSL Model Railway Guide 2 – Layout Planning.* Patrick Stephens Ltd

Bassett, C. 2014 *Hobbs Hill, Railway Modeller,* Volume 65, Number 761 March Edition, Pp 170–177. Peco Publications & Publicity Ltd

Beck, K.M. 1983 *The West Midland Lines of the GWR.* Ian Allan Ltd

Beck, K.M. 1986 *The Great Western North of Wolverhampton.* Ian Allan Ltd

Beck, K.M. & Harris, N. 1987 *GWR Reflections.* Silver Link Publishing Ltd

Biddle, G. & Nock, O.S. 1983 *The Railway Heritage of Britain.* Michael Joseph Ltd

Binns, D. 1987 *LNER / North Eastern Region Steam in Yorkshire.* Wyvern Publications

Bunce, C. 2011 *Great British Railway Journeys.* Harper Collins Publishers

Burkin, N. 2010 *Model Railway Layout Construction and Design Techniques.* The Crowood Press

Carter, E.F. 1950 *The Model Railway Encyclopaedia.* Burke Publishing Company

Cartwright, R. & Russell, R.T. 1981 *The Welshpool & Llanfair Light Railway.* David & Charles

Cooper, B.K. 1983 *Southern Railway Handbook.* Ian Allan Ltd

Cryer, G. 2014 *Shropshire Railways.* The Crowood Press

Freezer, C.J. 1991 *Model Railways – The Complete Guide to Designing, Building and Operating a Model Railway.* BCA.

Green, C.C. 1997 *Cambrian Railways 1859–1947 Combined Edition.* Ian Allan Ltd

Halligan, C. 2014 'Trefor', *Railway Modeller,* Volume 65, Number 764 June Edition, Pp 422–429. Peco Publications & Publicity Ltd

Hill, T. 2010 *Creating Realistic Landscapes for Model Railways.* The Crowood Press

Karau, P. 1977 *Great Western Branch Line Termini Volume 1.* Oxford Publishing Co.

Karau, P. 1978 *Great Western Branch Line Termini Volume 2.* Oxford Publishing Co.

Keyzer, M. & Dixon, R. 2014 'Rosehill', *Railway Modeller,* Volume 65, Number 770, December Edition, Pp 978-983. Peco Publications & Publicity Ltd

Lowery, D. 1993 *Advanced Model Railways.* The Apple Press

Mitchell, V. & Smith, K. 2009 *Branch Lines Around Oswestry (Gobowen, Tanat Valley, Llanfyllin and Welshpool).* Middleton Press

Mitchell, W. R. & Joy, D. 1982 *Settle to Carlisle. A Railway over the Pennines.* Dalesman Books

Prideaux, J.D.C.A. 1982 *The Welsh Narrow-Gauge Railway – A Pictorial History.* David & Charles

Pybus, R. 2015 *Designing and Building Model Railway Baseboards.* The Crowood Press

Scott, W.J. 1972 *The Great Great Western.* EP Publishing Ltd

Smith, M. 1995 *Portrait of the Central Wales Line.* Ian Allan Ltd

Tisdale, D.C. 2015 *Building OO-Gauge Wagons and Vans for Model Railways.* The Crowood Press

Vaughan, A. 1977 *A Pictorial Record of Great Western Architecture.* Oxford Publishing Co.

Williams, C.L. 1974 *Great Western Steam in Wales and the Border Counties.* D. Bradford Barton Ltd

Williams, C.L. 1976 *Great Western Branch Line Steam – Volume 1.* D. Bradford Barton Ltd

SUPPLIERS

The following suppliers are ones that I have used for kits, component parts and raw materials when constructing layouts. The materials should also be available via your local model shop, which might be your first port of call. I have no connection with the suppliers listed below, other than as a satisfied customer, and the list is not exhaustive.

NB: Scenic accessory items from suppliers such as Noch, Woodland Scenics, Silfur and MiniNatur are available from model shops rather than direct from the supplier.

51L Models/Wizard Models

Wizard Models
PO Box 70
Barton upon Humber
DN18 5XY
T: +44 (0) 1652 635885
E: Andrew@modelsignals.com
wizardmodels.co.uk
White-metal kits and components; brass kits

Ancorton Models

Distributed by a number of the larger retailers, such as Gaugemaster and Hattons
E: via web page link
ancortonmodels.com
Range of ready-to-plant and kit structures for N-gauge and OO-gauge

Cooper Craft

Broom Lane,
Oake
Taunton
TA4 1BE
T: +44 (0) 1823 461961
E: via web page link
cooper-craft.co.uk
Plastic wagon and van kits; plastic wagon and van components and underframe kits

Dart Castings

17 Hurst Close
Staplehurst
Tonbridge
Kent TN12 0BX
T: +44 (0) 1580 892917
E: enquiries@dartcastings.co.uk
dartcastings.co.uk
White-metal components; white-metal figures

Gaugemaster

Gaugemaster House
Ford Road
Arundel, West Sussex
BN18 0BN
T: +44 (0) 1903 884488
F: +44 (0) 1903 884377
E: via web page link
gaugemaster.com
Retailer and supplier of a wide range of materials and kits

K & S Metals

Distributed in the UK by:
J Perkins Distribution Ltd
Northdown Business Park
Ashford Road
Lenham
Kent ME17 2DL
T: +44 (0) 1622 854 300
F: +44 (0) 1622 854 301
E: sales@jpmodel.co.uk
ksmetals.com
Brass sheet and rod

Knightwing

Knightwing International
Malham Works
33 Almondbury Bank
Huddersfield
W.Yorks HD5 8HE
T: +44 (0) 1484 537191
E: sales@knightwing.co.uk
knightwing.co.uk
Plastic kits and white-metal components in N-gauge and OO-gauge

Metcalfe Kits
Bell Busk
Skipton
North Yorkshire BD23 4DU
T: +44 (0) 1729 830072
F: +44 (0) 1729 830074
E: info@metcalfemodels.com
metcalfemodels.com
Die-cut card building kits and ancillary structure kits in OO-gauge and N-gauge

Peco
Peco Technical Advice Bureau
Underleys
Beer
Devon EX12 3NA
T: +44 (0) 1297 21542
F: +44 (0) 1297 20229
E: info@pecobeer.co.uk
pecobeer.co.uk
Plastic kits

Plastruct
Available from local model shops
Extruded plastic components

Ratio Models
Distributed by Peco, see above
Plastic kits and components

Scalescenes
scalescenes.com
Online/downloadable detailed card kits in N-gauge and OO-gauge

Shire Scenes
The Old Armoury
North Street
Somerton
Somerset TA11 7NY
T: +44 (0) 1458 272446
E: order@shirescenes.co.uk
shirescenes.co.uk
Etched brass kits in N-gauge and OO-gauge

Slater's Plastikard Ltd
Old Road
Darley Dale
Matlock
Derbyshire DE4 2ER
T: +44 (0) 1629 734053
F: +44 (0) 1629 732235
E: slaters@slatersplastikard.com
slatersplastikard.com
Range of plain and embossed plasticard in varying thicknesses; micro-strip and plastic rod

Superquick Model Kits
16 Carlyle Road
Bristol BS5 6HG
T: +44 (0)117 230 0777
E: via web page link
superquick.co.uk
Range of card kits in OO-gauge

Ten Commandments
20 Struan Drive
Inverkeithing
Fife KY11 1AR
T: 01383 410032
E: tencommandants@cast-in-stone.co.uk
cast-in-stone.co.uk
Range of stone-cast detailing items for layouts and wagon loads for painting

Wills Kits
Distributed by Peco, see above
Plastic kits and components

INDEX